God
is my
Strength

FIFTY BIBLICAL
RESPONSES TO ISSUES
FACING WOMEN TODAY

Patricia A. Ennis

God is My Strength is a much needed resource for today's busy woman. Having worked with women in all seasons of life for over thirty years, I was excited to see the information that Dr Ennis is conveying to today's woman. It is very apparent that Dr Ennis has spent a lot of time with Christian women and knows the problems that they face. Her book is a treasure of information to help Christian women of all ages answer difficult life questions from a Biblical perspective and how to apply those Biblical principles in their lives daily. Women of all ages will benefit from the wisdom Dr Ennis brings to the problems that women face in the 21st Century.

Kenda Bartlett
Concerned Women for America, Executive Director

In this day of self-centered religion and cultural confusion, Pat Ennis offers cogent, practical answers for twenty-first century life. In *God is My Strength* Ennis directs women back to the assurances, promises and challenges found in Scripture. By applying the truths found in Ennis's book, women will grow deeper in faith, closer to God and more confident in living out their Christian faith in the world.

Jeanne Dennis
Host, Heritage of Truth TV
www.heritageoftruth.com

For many years the productivity of women has been undersold in the erroneous thinking that if it is not related to husband, children and home, it is thwarting her Godly purpose. Even a brief overview of Proverbs 31 disproves that viewpoint. God's kingdom is in dire need of the wisdom of His women educated and active in our culture – modeling His love for all mankind. How? This book is the primer!

Anne Hettinger
State Director for Concerned Women for America of Texas

As a counselor and professor of women's issues, this is a must read. Deep thinking, commonsensical and no nonsense truths about

God's answers are Pat Ennis's specialty. The timeless truths, great wisdom and insight within these pages are an excellent resource for anyone who counsels, teaches or interacts with women.

Glenda Hotton,
Counselor for Women, Professor of Women's Issues

What does a God-focused life really look like? When God is truly at the center of all you do, you'll experience His blessings and guidance as never before. *God Is My Strength* is about living wisely in His power instead of your own. If that's your heart's desire, you'll find this book to be a dear and constant companion.

Steve and Becky Miller
Christian Authors

These days, biblical womanhood is dismissed by popular Christian women writers as outdated, unattainable and even 'unbiblical'. But their quick judgments and distorted teachings leave young women like me feeling confused and ashamed of our feminine identity in Jesus Christ. Thankfully, Dr Pat Ennis wipes away the stereotypes and misleadings. Using Scripture as her foundation, Dr Ennis teaches women that biblical womanhood doesn't look like weakness or floral dress patterns, but intellect, courage and strength in the One who liberated us.

Chelsen Vicari
Author and Evangelical Action Director
at the Institute on Religion & Democracy

In her new book, *God Is My Strength*, Dr Ennis focuses on the problems facing women in the ever changing world of today, offering Godly advice in a number of areas that impact Christian women. Her book contains solid Biblical answers in a practical, readable volume. I highly recommend that 21st century women read *God Is My Strength*, and give it to their friends and family members."

Denise George,
Author, teacher, speaker www.denisegeorge.org

God is my Strength

FIFTY BIBLICAL
RESPONSES TO ISSUES
FACING WOMEN TODAY

Patricia A. Ennis

CHRISTIAN
FOCUS

Unless otherwise indicated, Scripture quotations are from the *Holy Bible, English Standard Version*, copyright © 2001 by Crossway Bibles, a division of Good News Publishers. Used by permission. All rights reserved.

Scripture quotations marked 'NASB' are from the *New American Standard Bible*, copyright © 1960, 1962, 1963, 1968, 1971, 1972, 1973, 1975, 1977, 1995 by The Lockman Foundation. Used by permission.

Scripture quotations marked 'NKJV' are from the *New King James Version*. Copyright © 1982 by Thomas Nelson Inc. Used by permission. All rights reserved.

Scripture quotations marked 'KJV' are from the *King James Version*.

Copyright © Patricia A. Ennis, 2015

paperback ISBN 978-1-78191-642-1
epub ISBN 978-1-78191-668-1
mobi ISBN 978-1-78191-669-8

Published in 2015
by
Christian Focus Publications Ltd.
Geanies House, Fearn, Ross-shire,
IV20 1TW, Scotland, UK
www.christianfocus.com

Cover design by
Pete Barnsley (Creative Hoot)
Printed by Bell and Bain, Glasgow

MIX
Paper from
responsible sources
FSC
www.fsc.org
FSC® C007785

All rights reserved. No part of this publication may be reproduced, stored in a retrieval system, or transmitted, in any form, by any means, electronic, mechanical, photocopying, recording or otherwise, without the prior permission of the publisher or a licence permitting restricted copying. In the U.K. such licences are issued by the Copyright Licensing Agency, Saffron House, 6-10 Kirby Street, London, EC1 8TS, www.cla.co.uk.

CONTENTS

MYSELF

MY HOME

MY WORLD

Dedicated to

My Pastor's Wife,
Selah Helms,
who daily models that God is her strength

and
Steve and Becky Miller

*for their support of my writing ministry and
consistent friendship throughout the years.*

ACKNOWLEDGEMENTS

I am indebted to the many individuals who supported the creation of **God Is My Strength**. *Among them I offer special gratitude to:*

Dr Tim LaHaye, John MacArthur and Paige Patterson—your vision to develop a character-based Home Economics curriculum and perpetuate it made this volume possible.

Carella DeVol—my best earthly friend. Your moral support, enthusiasm and consistent prayer on all aspects of my ministry are a constant source of blessing.

Catherine MacKenzie—your enthusiasm for **God Is My Strength** was evident from our initial contact. Thank you for personally meeting with me, presenting my proposal to the Editorial Committee, responding to a myriad of questions and for seeing the project through to its completion.

My Endorsers, who not only supported the content of **God Is My Strength** but my character.

The Christian Focus Team—your commitment to excellence made this partnership in the ministry of the written word a joy.

My Students at Christian Heritage College (now San Diego Christian), The Master's College and Southwestern Baptist Theological Seminary—your presence in my classes, completion of my assignments and choice to seek my counsel contributed to the compilation of this volume.

The Horner Homemaking House Team, Rebekah Swicegood, Christina Wilson and Ariel Youngbird—for your prayers, affirming words and encouraging smiles throughout the manuscript development.

My Heavenly Father—YOU established the criteria for living as a victorious Christian woman in Your Holy Word and then provided the strength to apply it to daily living. Eternity will not be long enough for me to express my love and gratitude to YOU!

FOREWORD

Dr Pat Ennis has given her life to educate young Christian women. As a college and seminary professor she has equipped countless faithful young women for lifetimes of joyful fruitful service to Christ in their singleness, in their marriages and in their careers. She has prepared them for motherhood and to reach their neighbors. She has held the bar high for them to serve with excellence in their church and in their workplace. I have known Pat for more than 30 years, during which time my wife and I have repeatedly observed her godly influence and Biblical impact upon college students, including our daughter and daughters-in law.

Jesus said, '*A pupil is not above his teacher; but everyone, after he has been fully trained, will be like his teacher.*' (Luke 6:40) Most important in Christian education is the character of the teacher. Dr Pat Ennis is a faithful woman of God worthy of emulation. '*... a woman who fears the LORD, she shall be praised ... let her works praise her in the gates.*' (Prov. 31:30-31)

This most helpful book calls upon the Word of God to carefully answer 50 vital questions that every young woman is facing today. Pat's loving approach engages their searching young hearts and minds. She sensitively relates practical answers, keen guidance and helpful approaches to steer them for a lifetime of honor to Christ. I whole-heartedly recommend *God Is My Strength: Biblical Responses to Questions Raised by Twenty-first Century Women* to every woman who desires to serve and glorify Christ in every dimension of her life.

Dr Bob Provost, President, Slavic Gospel Association

INTRODUCTION
How Do I Gain Strength for my Daily Journey?

Women often ask me, 'How do I gain strength for my daily journey?' Because I am by profession a Home Economics-Family and Consumer Scientist they generally expect a management based response. However, since I am a Christian first and a professional Home Economics-Family and Consumer Scientist second, my response is generally something like, 'the primary way to successfully gain strength for your daily journey is to acknowledge that God alone is your refuge and strength (Ps. 46). Only by reading, meditating upon, and applying His timeless Word to your life will you be able to navigate through the daily demands placed upon you.'

You and I do not have to demonstrate a lack of backbone, nor be like a rag doll that flops about if we choose to commit our way to the Lord and trust Him (Ps. 37). Rather, we are to exhibit strength under the control of the Holy Spirit by automatically casting our burdens on the Lord and allowing *Him* to sustain us (Ps. 55:22; Gal. 5:22-23). This type of reflex reaction demonstrates that we understand that we can complete all of the tasks He has assigned us to complete (Phil. 4:13).

God Is My Strength: Biblical Responses to Questions Raised by Twenty-first Century Women was written to allow you to spend time in your heavenly Father's company, cultivating character qualities that contribute to trusting God for your daily strength. The responses for the fifty questions comprising the book's contents are drawn from the spiritual challenges that I, as well as women I have taught and counseled through my spiritual pilgrimage, confront. As the unchanging Word of God is applied to our lives, we become victors rather than victims—and in the process, experience growth toward comprehending that God is *always* our strength (Ps. 29:11). The phrase 'Godly Woman in Progress' is used through the book to emphasize that God becomes a woman's strength when she understands and applies the truth found in His Word on a daily basis.

So I invite you to open your heart to the Scriptures—God's special instructions to His children. Saturate your mind with His thoughts, examine the lives of women who are recorded on the pages of His Word, and meditate on principles designed to assist you in developing the type of lifestyle that reflects that God is your strength regardless of your circumstances. I urge you to consider using the 'Sustaining Your Spiritual Stamina' projects found at the conclusion of each section to reinforce the truth that *God Is My Strength* teaches.

It is my prayer that *God Is My Strength: Biblical Responses to Questions Raised by Twenty-first Century Women* will launch for you a lifelong quest of developing character qualities that contribute to the development of a way of life which clearly reflects that God is your strength. Begin today and anticipate, with joy, the deepening of your relationship with your heavenly Father (Jer. 31:3).

Yours for the Journey,
Pat ☺

PHILIPPIANS 4:13, 19

MY FRIENDSHIPS

Am I Nurturing A Heart for Others?

1. What is a Friend?

When you think of defining the word *friend* what qualities come to mind? Do you consider actions, character traits, or a combination of both? As I asked myself this question I found my heart longing to be the kind of friend that pleases my heavenly Father. I knew that if I searched His Word He would help me understand friendship from His perspective, so I prayerfully began. My search led me to the study of biblical friendships—Ruth and Naomi (Ruth 1-4), David and Jonathan (1 Sam. 18-20; 2 Sam. 1, 9), and Mary and Elizabeth (Luke 1:39-56). Based on both the actions and character traits displayed by these biblical friendships, I created 'The Friendship Alphabet' as a guideline to integrating godly character traits into my friendships.

PAT'S FRIENDSHIP ALPHABET
A True Friend ...

*A*ccepts you the way you are.

*B*rings out your best.

*C*omes alongside when you encounter challenging circumstances.

*D*oesn't take advantage of your graciousness.

*E*ncourages you to reach your greatest potential.

*F*orgives your mistakes.

*G*ives to you instead of consistently expecting to receive.

*H*elps you whenever possible.

*I*nvites you to accompany her to a variety of activities and wants

*J*ust to 'be' with you.

*K*eeps in contact with you.

*L*oves you for who you are rather than the contribution
you can make to her life.

*M*akes an effort to be on time to all planned times together.

*N*ever judges you.

*O*ffers you encouragement.

*P*rays for you.

*Q*uickly expresses gratitude for the contribution you
make to her life.

*R*espects you even when she does not agree with you.

*S*ays affirming things about you.

*T*ells you the truth as she sees it.

*U*nderstands you have many other responsibilities.

*V*alues the privilege of being with you.

*W*aits to hear all of your thoughts before voicing her opinion.

X-plains the 'whys' of her behaviors.

*Y*ields her right to be in control and adds

*Z*est to your life.

May I encourage you to take the time to read these portraits of biblical friendships, create your own alphabet and then purpose, with our Lord's strength, to become a friend that pleases your heavenly Father? If you choose to do so, I believe that you will find, as I did, that in the midst of your demanding days, the depth and breadth of your friendships will increase.

2. Do I Have a Kindred Spirit?

Most of us long for a 'kindred spirit' friend such as the one so eloquently described by Anne Shirley in the classic story of an orphan girl, *Anne of Green Gables*:

> *I've dreamed of meeting her all my life …*
> *a bosom friend—an intimate friend, you know—a*
> *really kindred spirit to whom I can confide my inmost soul.*[1]

Her longing to find a 'kindred spirit' is replicated in the hearts of women because, as Ecclesiastes 4:9-12 teaches, we all have a built-in need for companionship.

Many research studies reinforce what Anne Shirley and Solomon, the author of Ecclesiastes 4:9-12, taught centuries ago: 'Two are better than one, because they have a good reward for their labor. For if they fall, one will lift up his companion. But woe to him who is alone when he falls, for he has no one to help him up.' Take, for example, the findings of the landmark UCLA study:

---

1. Lucy Maud Montgomery, *Anne of Green Gables* (Boston: L.C. Page and Publishers, 1940), 75.

3

✳ Friends help us live better and longer.

✳ Within the UCLA study, the famed Nurses' Health Study
   from Harvard Medical School was cited; it found that
   the more friends women had, the less likely they were to
   develop physical impairments as they aged, and the more
   likely they were to lead joyful lives. In fact, the results were
   so significant, the researchers concluded, that not having
   close friends or confidantes was as detrimental to one's
   health as smoking or carrying extra weight.

✳ When researchers evaluated how well women functioned
   after the death of their spouse, they found that even in
   the midst of the biggest of life's stressors, women who had
   a close friend and confidante were more likely to survive
   the experience without any new physical impairment or
   permanent loss of vitality. Those without friends were not
   always so fortunate.[2]

I would encourage you, as you consider Ecclesiastes 4:9-12
and these research findings, to ask yourself if you are cultivating and nourishing relationships that will strengthen your
spiritual and physical health. Though gaining proficiency
in life skills is essential for life in the twenty-first century,
do not sacrifice the nurturing of a heart for others on the
altar of your 'to do' list. Today, plan to contact at least
one friend as a part of your busy schedule—you will
be thankful that you did. Concurrently take the time to
nurture the most important friendship that you will ever
have—that of a relationship with your Lord (Prov. 18:24).

2. Found at www.isismedica.com/Friendship

3. Am I A Trustworthy Friend?

If an intimate friend were to describe you, would she use the word *trustworthy*? What would be the basis of their description? Do you nurture security, love, service, freedom, enjoyment, faith and encouragement in your relationship? Do you challenge your friend to reach her full potential?[3] If so, you have the foundation of being a *trustworthy* friend.

A brief journey through Scripture reveals the significant impact that trustworthy friends can make on your life. Friends, according to Scripture ...

* refresh one another (Prov. 11:25).

* greatly influence us (Prov. 13:20).

* love you enough to share information you don't want to hear in a way that you can accept it (Prov. 16:21).

* refuse to entertain the words of a slanderer (Prov. 16:28).

* are often more loyal than family members (Prov. 18:24).

* help you to see where you fall short of doing God's will (Prov. 27:6).

* offer wise counsel because their overriding motive is to seek your long-term good (Prov. 27:9).

* are available in time of need (Prov. 27:10).

* choose to be reconciled to one another before attempting to worship their heavenly Father (Matt. 5:24).

---

3. See Pat Ennis and Lisa Tatlock, *Becoming a Woman Who Pleases God, A Guide to Developing Your Biblical Potential* (Chicago: Moody, 2003), 26-27.

✳ forgive one another (Matt. 6:14).

✳ reveal their relationship with God by their interaction with you. Consider the encouragement of John 13:35, 'by this all people will know that you are my disciples, if you have love one to another.'

✳ potentially mold your life toward wisdom (1 Cor. 15:33).

✳ encourage, challenge and hold you accountable (Gal. 6:2).

✳ meet your needs in specific ways (Gal. 6:10).

✳ speak the truth in love (Eph. 4:15).

✳ help you see the true, honorable, right, pure, lovely, excellent and praiseworthy qualities of life (Phil. 4:8-9).

✳ are a visible example of God's sacrificial love toward mankind (John 13:34-35; 1 John 4:7).

A trustworthy friend has an understanding, encouraging, sympathetic and tactful spirit. As well, she has the ability to retain another's confidence (Prov. 10:19). As I counsel with women who have trouble in applying *trustworthiness* to their speech, I encourage them to say, 'Stop, please do not tell me that—I am not trustworthy!' when someone begins to share information they know they cannot refrain from passing on. I find they do not need to repeat the phrase many times before their speech habits change.

Align Your Thoughts

So, according to Scripture's standard, are you a *trustworthy* friend? Consider writing each of the statements above in a question, record your response, and ask your heavenly

Father to increase your level of *trustworthiness* ... here's one to get you started:

Are my friends refreshed when they spend time with me?

4. What is My Friendship Confidence Score?

As a twenty-first century consumer, I am well aware of my credit score—a high one opens multiple financial options, while a low one can quickly diminish them. As a friend, when I consider the *friendship confidence score* that I should build, I am reminded of Elizabeth, the mother of John the Baptist[4] (Luke 1:39-56). Her life teaches us much about the confidence that should be evident in our relationships. See how she responded to her young friend and cousin, Mary, who was experiencing personal challenges.

A vignette of Elizabeth ...
Elizabeth was the wife of Zacharias the priest (Luke 1:5-7). Luke 1:6 reports that 'they were both upright before God, walking blamelessly in all the commandments and statutes of the Lord'—certainly a foundational quality for our *Friendship Confidence Score*. At the time Mary chose to visit Elizabeth both were faced with challenging pregnancies— Elizabeth was what today would be diagnosed as high risk because of her age (Luke 1:7), while Mary was unwed (Luke 1:26-38). Additionally, Elizabeth chose to seclude herself for the first five months of her pregnancy; the absence of friends and family and the presence of a husband who had

---

4. A helpful resource is *Elizabeth, Lessons on Grace and Faith from the Life of an Older Woman* by Nancy Leigh DeMoss. Visit the Revive Our Hearts website for ordering information (http://www.LifeAction.org).

been struck dumb in the temple because of his unbelief at Gabriel's announcement (Luke 1:18-25) all paved the way for Elizabeth to warmly welcome Mary (Luke 1:39-56).

God knew that Elizabeth and Mary needed one another! During the three months they spent together they undoubtedly nurtured one another for the incredibly painful events that would later impact their lives. John the Baptist would be beheaded for speaking boldly against Herod's adulterous relationship with his brother's wife (Matt. 14:1-12), while Mary would bear the unspeakable pain of watching the crucifixion of Jesus (Luke 23:26-49; John 19:18, 23-30).

Elizabeth demonstrates friendship through:

* *Availability.* Mary had confidence that she would be welcome in Elizabeth's home—Mary had no way of alerting Elizabeth to her intention to come for a three-month visit (Luke 1:39-40).

* *A patient spirit.* Elizabeth waited for Mary to share the reason for her visit rather than immediately interrogating her or preempting the situation by sharing her good news (Luke 1:40b-41).

* *A clean vessel.* Elizabeth was a clean vessel that the Holy Spirit could use to affirm the Lord's work in Mary's life (Luke 1:41). At Mary's arrival two astonishing actions occurred—John the Baptist literally leapt in his mother's womb, and Elizabeth was filled with the Holy Spirit and began to prophesy (Luke 1:41-45).

* *A heart for hospitality.* Elizabeth offered extended hospitality to Mary (Luke 1:56); since Mary arrived when Elizabeth was six months pregnant, she evidently stayed until John the

Baptist was born—not necessarily the most convenient time for a long-term guest!

Friendship is one of the most precious of God's gifts to us.

May I encourage you to evaluate your friendships in relation through the same factors?

Friendship Confidence Score Factors

* Am I available?

* Do I have a patient spirit?

* Am I a clean vessel?

* Do I have a heart for hospitality?

Align Your Thoughts

As you seek to build friendships, ask your gracious heavenly Father to provide you with the strength to mold your character so that you are able to provide 'yes' responses to the *Friendship Confidence Score Factors* (Phil. 4:13). Consider adding some additional ones to the list from your study of the Scriptures.

5. How Can I Cultivate Healthy Friendships?

Who wants to have anemic friendships? I surely do not; however, if I want to cultivate healthy friendships, I will need to seek God's strength to invest my time, energy, and resources into them. Read 2 Corinthians 9:6 as it provides a simple agrarian principle—the harvest one receives is directly proportionate to the amount and quality of seed sown. Galatians 6:7-10 reminds us that we will reap what we sow. Bible teacher John MacArthur helps us understand this passage by stating, 'our love for fellow Christians is the primary test of our love for God.'[5] Let's take the time to consider some principles that assist us in the healthy cultivation of our friendships:

✳ Take the time to genuinely know your friends. This means learning how to share yourself intimately and appropriately, sharing at the same level of disclosure your friend is sharing, moving into intimate sharing slowly, and exhibiting a willingness to share strengths and weaknesses, failures and fears, as well as victories and successes.

✳ Wholeheartedly listen to the person when she is speaking—even if you think she is going to tell you something you do not want to hear. Often when a friend begins to communicate something we are not excited about knowing, our first reaction is to begin to build our defense rather than to listen to her entire conversation.

✳ Be trustworthy; the first quality of the wise woman (Prov. 31:11-12) is that she 'does good, not harm.' While placed in the context of the marriage relationship, the principle is the same for all relationships—you are to do all that is in your power to improve the person's life, seek to help her develop her potential to the fullest, and not compete, but assist the person in doing the work and will of God. Refusing to 'do harm' includes defending your friend, never betraying or slandering her, seeking to keep promises, never sharing with others what she has shared with you in confidence, or breaking her spirit by unnecessary criticism. You will also not desert her by withdrawing your acceptance of her. Do not

---

5. John MacArthur, *The MacArthur Study Bible* (Nashville: Word: 1997), note at Galatians 6:10.

make your agreement conditional upon her cooperating with you or conforming to your standards. And do not withdraw your interest or care when you do not have an immediate need for her in your life. If a woman cannot be a trustworthy friend, it is also unlikely she will be a trustworthy spouse since 'practice makes perfect'.

* Practice consistency in your relationships—even when you do not feel like it. If you are going to follow the biblical model for friendships, you will choose to 'love at all times' (Prov. 17:17). This means that your warmth toward your friends is to be unwavering, and you choose to regularly communicate that you care about them—even when you do not approve of their choices.

* Work hard to ensure you are doing your part to maintain the relationship. When you neglect to invest time and effort in a relationship you are essentially saying, 'I don't care very much.' Maintaining the relationships suggests that you are a forgiving person (Col. 3:13-14) willing to bear with weaknesses and idiosyncrasies of others (1 Cor. 13:7) and quick to clear up misunderstandings as soon as they arise (Gal. 6:1). It also means dealing with your pride and asking forgiveness when you have offended your friend (Matt. 5:23-24; 6:14-15) and surrendering your desire to punish her when she has hurt or upset you (2 Tim. 2:23-26). True friendship freely grants forgiveness (Eph. 4:31-32) and forgets the transgression (Ps. 103:12; Jer. 31:34).

Do you want to cultivate healthy friendships? If so, you will seek God's strength to invest your time, energy and resources in them (Phil. 4:13).

6. What Does a Maturing Friendship Look Like?

What are the similarities between roses and friendships? Your first thought may be nothing—yet if you take the time to develop the idea a number of resemblances surface. Just as the beauty of the unfurling rose remains concealed until it is fully open, so often the loveliness of a friendship remains undiscovered until you create many memories. Since you have a busy schedule, you will probably not experience the same level of intimacy in each friendship you cultivate. Perhaps the visual image of a budding rose will help you understand the various phases of friendship.

PHASE ONE—THE GREEN BUD

As with the rose when it is wrapped in its green shroud, the knowledge of your friend is vague at *Green Bud* phase. You know who the person is and perhaps some basic information about her. Our wise heavenly Father brings a variety of temperaments together to sharpen one another in friendships (Prov. 27:17). Sometimes the friends will be very similar; other times they will be very different. Regardless of the temperaments of the ladies, the *Green Bud* phase begins with respect for one another. Though one of the ladies will probably need to initiate the relationship, the other can demonstrate that she is available.

PHASE TWO—THE EMERGING BUD

It is always exciting to observe the green shroud slowly unfold to reveal the potential beauty of the rose petals; experience teaches that if you preempt the process by your unsolicited assistance the petals may emerge earlier, but often are damaged. The same is true in budding friendships—time and patience are necessary for the *Green Bud* phase to transition to the *Emerging Bud* phase. Characteristic of the *Emerging Bud* phase is knowing more about your friend, her interests, what she does and does not enjoy doing, perhaps some future goals and a bit about her past. Essentially, you know not only who she is but also what she is like. Though you may do things together—perhaps work together, talk about interests together and occasionally ask one another for help—generally there is little commitment or much deep, intimate sharing.

PHASE THREE—THE UNFURLED ROSE

Given the proper climate and conditions, the *Emerging Bud* phase gently opens up to reveal the depth of the relationship distinctive of the *Unfurled Rose* phase. The true character of the friendship comes forth in this phase since you know your friend in greater depth. You have committed to spending time together and intimate sharing has occurred. Characteristics of the *Unfurled Rose* phase are a variety of shared interests, with similar values; the friends assume mutual responsibility to keep the relationship on track and growing. Nourishment is characteristic of the *Unfurled Rose* phase. Verna Birkey writes in *Women Connecting with Women*: 'Nourishment, then, is something that feeds my soul hunger so that life will be full, healthy and growing, instead of fainting and ebbing away.'[6] Within this phase the ladies offer nourishment to

---

6. Verna Birkey, *Women Connecting with Women* (Mukileto: WinePress Publishing, 1998), 54.

one another through affirmation, spiritual and emotional encouragement, and, when necessary, admonition and reproof.

PHASE FOUR—THE FULL-BLOWN ROSE

The genuine charm of a rose is discovered when it is full-blown; likewise, the authenticity of a friendship is revealed in the *Full-Blown* phase of a relationship. Every now and then rose buds will start out healthy but will droop or their petals shatter before they reach their maximum potential. The same is true in friendships—all will not mature into the *Full-Blown* phase. However, those that do achieve this level of maturity enjoy the unique quality of commitment which is the foundation of the *Full-Blown* phase. You will enjoy the continued benefits of the *Green, Emerging* and the *Unfurled Rose* phases; but it is commitment that prompts you to endure with your friend when she is preoccupied, is experiencing difficulty or has failed. It means 'hanging in there' under all circumstances, and 'staying with it' when the well of spontaneous affection seems nearly dry. Ultimately it is a commitment to your friend's highest good—regardless of personal cost. Love and reciprocal contribution encourage the *Full-Blown* phase to flourish (Eccles. 4:9-12). Warmth, communication of mutual concern and respect, and a willingness to accept one another demonstrate the presence of love. When each of you contribute to the maintenance of the relationship it will continue to grow. Extending kindness to one another, forgiving one another (Eph. 4:32), bearing with weaknesses and idiosyncrasies (Gal. 6:1-2), and reassuring one another will ensure that there are no weeds in your Garden of Friendship.

Align Your Thoughts

Has a busy schedule robbed you of the incredible blessings of cultivating healthy relationships? Regardless of your answer, may I encourage you to invest time, energy, and resources to either develop or nurture them? A profuse friendship garden will most likely come forth if you choose to do so!

7. How Can I Weed My Friendship Garden?

Do you have weeds in your friendship garden? Perhaps yes, perhaps no; however, in the midst of our full days we can often overlook them until they begin to dominate. Since female companionship counters so many of the negative aspects of life, keeps you healthy and may even add years to your life, it is incredibly important to consistently examine the garden and weed it, if necessary. This not only helps to modify our own 'weedy' behavior but also allows us to graciously assist our friends in understanding their destructive effects on the relationship (Prov. 27:17).

The most important element in the fight against weeds is to promote the best environment possible for the growth of desirable plants. Improper watering or fertilization, soil compaction, insect damage, disease, poor drainage and improper sunlight are all conditions that increase the potential for weed development.[7] What is true of the care and maintenance of gardens is equally true in the nurturing of your friendships; relational weeds in the Friendship Garden have the potential of stunting or completely stopping growth. The book of John teaches that:

---

7. Found at http://www.lowes.com

✳ Loving others is a visual illustration of our discipleship (13:34-35).

✳ Christians exemplify that they are friends with Christ when they love one another (15:14).

✳ Christians are to love one another as Christ loved them (15:12).

✳ Loving one another is a command, not a suggestion, for Christians (15:17).

A variety of weeds can hinder the flourishing of love in the Friendship Garden including:

The Turned-Head Weed

The Turned-Head Weed grows in one direction while its head faces the opposite direction. It might be called the 'if only' weed because it lives on memories of other friendships and experiences. It damages existing relationships by its continual reference to other, 'more prosperous' relationships or by possessing unrealistic expectations of current ones. This weed is best eradicated by thanking God for precious memories and concentrating on nurturing the current relationships He provides (Eph. 5:20; Phil. 3:13; 1 Thess. 5:18).

The I-Me Weed

The I-Me Weed grows to enormous heights until nothing else in the garden can be seen; it is a real love-choker, often turning friendships into thickets of fighting and competition. The presence of this weed creates an environment directly opposite to the *agape* love commanded by God that challenges you to accept your friend exactly as she is, forgives and forgets unintentional slights, places no demands on the friendship, and allows the will rather than the emotions to control it. Another name for selfishness, the *I-Me Weed* quickly establishes itself as the center of the Friendship Garden and demands to be in control. It is most effectively eradicated by sowing the *Our-We* seed in the Friendship Garden (Prov. 13:10; Gal. 5:15, 19-25; Phil. 2:3; James 3:16).

The Clam-up Weed

The Clam-up Weed is one of the most difficult to eradicate because when one friend 'clams up' it is almost impossible to correct the situation; should this weed invade, the silence that falls over the Friendship Garden is like the silence of a tomb. The residual effect of this weed is often a suppression of one's feelings that may eventually erupt in an explosion; to eradicate, communicate frequently and temper the tone, choice and number of your words. Should disagreements arise, refuse to remain angry and be willing to admit your contribution to the conflict (Prov. 25:11, 26:20, 31:26; Eph. 4:15, 25-32).

The Wandering Affection Weed

The Wandering Affection Weed is small, ugly and has sharp leaves and roots that cut the roots of love, under the surface, out of sight, so a relationship does not know what is happening until it is too late. This weed seeks to cultivate a new relationship by destroying an existing one. *The Wandering Affection Weed* whispers slanderous comments about existing friends, suggests that she can best fulfill your friendship needs and insinuates that it is permissible to abort a long-established friendship for a new one with her. While it is important to pursue new friendships, it is not appropriate for you to undermine a deeply rooted friendship in order to do so. Eradication of *the Wandering Affection Weed* includes refusing to discredit an existing friendship, purposing to 'love at all times,' seeking to bear your friend's burdens, doing things which are particularly pleasing to her and concentrating on her positive qualities rather than her weaknesses (Ps.101:5; Prov. 6:16-19, 17:17; Gal. 6:2, 10; Phil. 4:8, 9).

The I Am Always Right Weed

Standing stiff and erect in the Friendship Garden, *The I Am Always Right Weed* offers a sharp, immediate response to anything she disagrees with; a pro at conflict, it is amazing that so many ugly words can spew forth from her lips if she is provoked. When she assumes this stance engaging in discussion with her is futile since she is always right. Eradication of the *I Am Always Right Weed* requires prayer on your part so that the words of your mouth and the meditations of your heart are acceptable to the Lord. Two ways to remove this weed from your friendship garden are:

✳ Filling your mind with God's Word so that your responses are His responses.

✳ Being willing to graciously and gently speak the truth in love so as to ensure you are not providing ammunition that keeps a conflict in momentum (Ps. 19:14, 39:1, 49:3, 119:11; Prov. 4:23-24, 10:20, 12:18, 15:2, 18:21, 21:23, 23:7, 25:11,

31:26; Matt. 12:33-37; Luke 6:45; Eph. 4:15; Col. 3:16; James 1:26-27, 3:6-10).

The I Call You When I Need You Weed

The I Call You When I Need You Weed lies dormant for long periods and then suddenly appears. The *I Call You When I Need You Weed* extracts from the friendship what she desires then allows it to lay latent until another need arises. As with the *I-Me Weed*, selfishness is the primary source of the *I Call You When I Need You Weed*. Eradication of this weed includes choosing to love your friend as yourself, being more concerned about her needs than yours, and praying for a heart that desires to honor others (Lev. 19:18; Matt. 5:43; Mark 12:33; Rom. 2:6-8, 12:10, 13:7; Phil. 2:3-4; Heb. 13:1; 2 Pet. 1:7-11).

Regardless of the appearance of these weeds, all generate from the same taproot: pride, the first of the six things that the Lord hates (Prov. 6:16-17). Pride cultivates disharmony in the Friendship Garden while humility, the opposite of pride, generates an atmosphere of peace and harmony (Col. 3:12-17). The most effective time to eradicate weeds in the Friendship Garden is when they are young, tender and actively growing—and you can only do this in the Lord's strength. As James 4:6, the spiritual weed killer, is applied to the invading weeds, your Friendship Garden will produce spectacular bouquets!

Align Your Thoughts

The Lord pleads in John 17:20-21, 'I do not pray for these alone, but also for those who will believe in Me through their word; that they all may be one, as You, Father, are in Me, and I in You; that they also may be one in Us, that the world may believe that You sent me' (NKJV). Are you quick to eradicate weeds from your Friendship Garden so that the watching world observes the love of God in your friendships?

8. Does A Portrait of Biblical Friendship Exist?

I enjoy studying the lives of men and women of the Bible because they allow me to see a practical application of Scripture (or not as the case may be).

Read: 1 Corinthians 10:1-12.

This is a reminder that every event recorded in Scripture was written for 'our instruction'—so it seems reasonable that we would look to biblical friendships as a guide for ours. One of the classic descriptions of friendship recorded in Scripture is that of Jonathan and David (1 Sam. 18:1-4; 19:1-7; 20:1-42; 23:16; 2 Sam. 1:17). The qualities of their relationship, as seen in the book of 1 Samuel, provide a wonderful role model for multi-tasked women:

* *Friendship requires effort* (18:1). In our twenty-first century society, too many friendships are based on surface attributes and selfish ambitions. Jonathan's cultivation of his friendship with David reflects a willingness to cross social barriers and personal agendas to develop a genuine relationship.

* *Friendship involves sacrifice* (18:4; 23:16-17). Unselfishness is always necessary to practice true friendship. Each individual must be willing to give up something treasured; in Jonathan's case, he willingly surrendered his rightful position as king.

* *Friendship promotes the best interests of the other* (19:1-7). Jeopardizing his own safety and relationship with his father,

Jonathan sought to alert David to potential danger, defended him and cultivated a spirit of reconciliation between Saul and David.

* *Friendship is willing to take the brunt of another person's circumstances* (20:24-33). Every woman needs someone to 'go to the wall' for her and, against insurmountable odds, Jonathan did 'go to the wall' for David.

Read: 2 Samuel 1:26

This clearly describes that David's love for Jonathan was reciprocated. 'A deep concern and affection was the basis of the covenantal relationship between Jonathan and David. This is the affection commanded by God when He said, "Love your neighbor as yourself."'[8]

May I encourage you to evaluate the qualities of Jonathan and David's friendship in light of the qualities resident in yours? Perhaps these questions will help ...

* Am I willing to pursue a relationship if it requires effort?

* Do I make significant personal sacrifices for my friends?

* Do I promote the best interests of my friends?

* Am I willing to take the brunt of another person's circumstances?

The writings of two authors—one from the twentieth century and one from the twenty-first—offer meaningful thoughts that aid women in focusing on the importance of

---

8. John MacArthur, *The MacArthur Study Bible* (Nashville: Word: 1997), note at 1 Samuel 20:17.

cherishing our friendships. Would your friends be able to write a comparable tribute to you?

> And a youth said, Speak to us of Friendship.
>
> And he answered, saying:
>
> Your friend is your needs answered. He is your field which you sow with love and reap with thanksgiving.
>
> And he is your board and your fireside.
>
> For you come to him with your hunger, and you seek him for peace.
>
> When your friend speaks his mind you fear not the 'nay' in your own mind, nor do you withhold the 'aye'. And when he is silent your heart ceases not to listen to his heart;
>
> For without words, in friendship, all thoughts, all desires, all expectations are born and shared, with joy that is unclaimed. When you part from your friend, you grieve not; for that which you love most in him may be clearer in his absence, as the mountain to the climber is clearer from the plain.
>
> And let there be no purpose in friendship save the deepening of the spirit. For love that seeks aught but the disclosure of its own mystery is not love but a net cast forth: and only the unprofitable is caught.
>
> And let your best be for your friend. If he must know the ebb of your tide, let him know its flood also. For what is your friend that you should seek him with hours to kill? Seek him always with hours to live. For it is his to fill your need, but not your emptiness. And in the sweetness of friendship let there be laughter, and sharing of pleasures.
>
> For in the dew of little things the heart finds its morning and is refreshed.[9]
>
> KAHLIL GIBRAN

---

9. Kahlil Gibran, *The Prophet* (New York: Alfred A. Knoph, Inc.: 1923), 58.

MY GREATEST PRIZE

It seems as each year ends,
I look back and think of my friends,
What I did right what I did wrong,
Who came into my life and who is gone.

But every year there are those who remain,
Looking only for friendship nothing else to gain.
They have stayed by me through good and bad,
Smiled when I am happy held me when I've been sad.

After so many years you begin to realize,
That a friend is life's greatest prize,
Not the pot of gold at the end of a rainbow,
That we seem to seek wherever we go.

So as I grow older and begin another New Year's Day,
I will thank God for those friends He sent my way.
And my New Year's resolution will always be,
To thank Him again for every breath of life He's given me.

Then I will pray He will show me the way,
Give me wisdom and guide me through each day.
And most of all at the end of each year,
Keep by me those friends I will always hold so dear.
And as I make new friends I'll treasure the old,
For the first are silver the latter gold.

JANET RITCHIE © 2002
USED BY PERMISSION

9. Is There A Stretegy for Me to Cherish My Friendships?

Only God can really know what you are truly like—the remainder of those with whom you interact must be satisfied with what they see and hear from you (1 Sam. 16:7). The woman who seeks to cultivate friendships that please her heavenly Father chooses, through His strength, to carefully evaluate the characteristics of her friendships against the unchanging wisdom found in His Word. This question was crafted to help you aerate the soil of your Friendship Garden by searching the Scriptures for *friendship wisdom* and then evaluating your garden's quality against God's ageless standards. Simply follow these instructions:

* Read the category and each Scripture listed under it.

* Copy and answer the questions developed for you; provide specific examples to support your yes or no response.

* Read each additional Scripture and rewrite it into a question that provides a basis for you to evaluate your performance as a friend.

* Seek your own Scriptures to augment those provided for you.

* Answer each question you wrote.

What kind of friend am I admonished to be?

* Do I love my friends at *all* times? (Prov. 17:17)

* Am I available to my friends when they are experiencing difficult times? (Prov. 18:24b)

* Suggested Scriptures for your questions: Proverbs 27:6; 1 Corinthians 13:7; Galatians 5:14.

What can ruin a friendship?

* Do I gossip about or slander my friends? (Prov. 16:28; 26:20)

* Do I intentionally share information with others who are neither part of the situation or the solution? (Prov. 17:9)

* Suggested Scriptures for your questions: Proverbs 20:19; Psalm 15:2; Matthew 7:1-5.

What kind of friend do we need?

* Do I have a friend who is more loyal than a family member? Do I display that kind of loyalty in my friendships? (Prov. 18:24)

* Do I have friends who exhibit the fruit of the Spirit? Do I exhibit the fruit of the Spirit in my dealings with my friends? (Gal. 5:22)

* Suggested Scriptures for your questions: Ephesians 4:1-6, 29.

Who wants to be that friend?

* Do I have a personal relationship with Jesus Christ? (John 15:14-15)

* Am I willing to invest the same energy to cultivate a strong friendship with Jesus Christ as I invest in earthly friendships? (Matt. 10:37)

* Suggested Scriptures for your questions: Proverbs 17:17b; John 15:13; 1 John 3:13-18.

Those who are not my friends

* How am I to respond to those with whom I do not share a compatible relationship? (Matt. 5:44)

* What type of behavior am I to manifest among those with whom I do not share a compatible relationship? (Rom. 12:17-21)

* Suggested Scriptures for your questions: Psalm 143; Proverbs 25:21-22.

My friendships with fellow Christians

✳ How should I treat other Christians? (Rom. 12:10)

✳ What must I guard against with fellow Christians?
(Rom. 14:10-13)

✳ Suggested Scriptures for your questions: Matthew 7:1-2, 5;
Philippians 2:3-4.

Making amends

✳ When others have wronged me, what must be my attitude?
(Matt. 6:12-15)

✳ When I have wronged others, what steps am I to take?
(Matt. 5:23-24)

✳ Suggested Scriptures for your questions: Matthew 18:21-22;
James 5:16.

Heart search.

✳ Is there someone I hold a grudge against? (Mark 11:25-26)

✳ Am I self-righteous or judgmental? (Luke 6:37-38)

✳ Suggested Scriptures for your questions: Matthew 5:38-42;
James 3:13-18.

Producing a profuse rose garden begins with the purchase
of a variety of healthy plants, is sustained with careful
irrigation and nutrition, pruned when appropriate and
weeded regularly. Though your favorite color of rose in
your Friendship Garden is a personal preference, each

color, according to All American Rose Selections,[10] expresses a specific sentiment. As you consider the qualities resident in the friendship you extend to others in light of the 'Color and Symbolism of Popular Roses' chart, would you conclude that you have cultivated a multicolored Friendship Bouquet?

COLOR AND SYMBOLISM OF POPULAR ROSES	
COLOR	SYMBOLISM
Red	Love, respect
Deep pink	Gratitude, appreciation
Light pink	Admiration, sympathy
White	Reverence, humility
Yellow	Joy, gladness, sociability, friendship
Orange	Enthusiasm, desire
Red and yellow	Gaiety, joviality

As you consider the response to this question perhaps the bit of prose that follows will assist you in affirming those you consider a part of your Friendship Garden.

Tribute
I love you not only for what you are,
but for what I am when I am with you.
I love you not only for what you have made of yourself,
but for what you are making of me.
I love you for the part of me that you bring out.

---

10. Found at www.rose.org/site/epage/13599. The All American Rose Selections is a non-profit association of rose growers dedicated to the introduction and promotion of exceptional roses.

I love you for putting your hands into my heaped-up heart, and passing over all the foolish and frivolous and weak things which you cannot help dimly seeing there, and for drawing out into the light all the beautiful, radiant belongings that no one else had looked quite far enough to find.

I love you for ignoring the possibilities of the fool
and weakling in me, and
For laying firm hold on the possibilities of good in me.
I love you for closing your eyes to the discords in me, and for
adding to the music in me by worshipful listening.

I love you because you are helping me to make of the lumber of my life not a tavern, but a Temple, and of the words of my every day not a reproach but a song.

I love you because you have done more than any creed could have done to make me good, and more than any fate could have done to make me happy.
You have done it just by being yourself.
Perhaps that is what being a friend means after all.[11]

Meditation Thoughts on My Friendships

The woman who trusts God as her strength ...

✳ builds relationships that deepen because she seeks to sharpen her friends spiritually and intellectually (Prov. 27:17; 31:28-29).

✳ when she speaks, has the ability to be firm, yet kind (Prov. 27:9b, 31:26).

---

11. Author unknown.

✳ speaks words that are encouraging, sympathetic, and tactful (Prov. 25:11).

✳ has the ability to keep another's confidence (Prov. 31:11-12).

✳ chooses words that bring comfort, hope, cheer and, when necessary, correction to her friends (Prov. 31:18; Gal. 6:10).

✳ is willing to share her most valuable asset—her time—with her friends (Prov. 31:18).

✳ acknowledges that she needs to cultivate female friendships (Eccles. 4:9-12).

✳ is more concerned about the quality of friendship she extends to others than what her friends can do for her (John 13:34-35).

✳ nurtures her friendships—one of God's most precious gifts to her—and purposes to not sacrifice the deepening of relationships on the altar of her 'to do' list (John 15:13).

✳ conscientiously cultivates the soil of her friendships (Gal. 6:1-2; Eph. 4:32; 1 Thess. 5:14).

✳ consistently weeds her Friendship Garden (James 4:6).

✳ uses the qualities of Jonathan and David as a role model for her friendships (1 Sam. 18:4; 19:1-7; 20:1-42; 23:16; 2 Sam. 1:17).

Building My Spiritual Stamina

Continually think about or contemplate the Scriptures that focus your mind on the qualities that promote godly friendships (cf. PHIL. 4:8)

A friend loves at all times,
and a brother is born for adversity.
PROVERBS 17:17

A man of many companions may come to ruin,
but there is a friend who sticks closer than a brother.
PROVERBS 18:24

Faithful are the wounds of a friend;
profuse are the kisses of an enemy.
PROVERBS 27:6

Oil and perfume make the heart glad,
and the sweetness of a friend comes from his earnest counsel.
Do not forsake your friend and your father's friend,
and do not go to your brother's house in the day of calamity.
PROVERBS 27:9-10

Iron sharpens iron,
and one man sharpens another.
PROVERBS 27:17

Two are better than one, because they have a good reward for
their toil.
For if they fall, one will lift up his fellow.
But woe to him who is alone when he falls and has not
another to lift him up!
Again, if two lie together, they keep warm,
but how can one keep warm alone?
And though a man might prevail against one who is alone,
two will withstand him—a threefold cord
is not quickly broken.
ECCLESIASTES 4:9-12

A new commandment I give to you,
that you love one another:
just as I have loved you, you also are to love one another.
By this all people will know that you are my disciples,
if you have love for one another.
JOHN 13:34-35

Do not be deceived:
Bad company ruins good morals.
1 CORINTHIANS 15:33

Bear one another's burdens, and so fulfill the law of Christ.
GALATIANS 6:2

So then, as we have opportunity, let us do good to everyone,
and especially to those who are the household of faith.
GALATIANS 6:10

Beloved, let us love one another,
for love is from God,
and whoever loves has been born of God and knows God.
1 JOHN 4:7

Sustaining My Spiritual Stamina

Further study to encourage renewal of your
mind and spirit (cf. EPH. 4:17-32)

✳ Search the Scriptures for behaviors that a friend should practice (Eph. 5:21; Col. 3:13; 1 Thess. 5:11, 14 will get you started).

✳ Learn the secret of a woman who chose to be a friend who loved at all times by exploring the life of Elizabeth, the mother of John the Baptist, in Luke 1:39-56.

31

✳ Develop your own *Friendship Confidence Score Factors* using the ones in 'What is My Friendship Confidence Score?' as a guide.

✳ Search the Scriptures for verses that align with the 'symbolism' column of the Color and Symbolism of Popular Roses table. Prepare your own table following the model below:

COLOR AND SYMBOLISM OF POPULAR ROSES		
COLOR	SYMBOLISM	SCRIPTURE REFERENCES
Red	Love, respect	
Deep pink	Gratitude, appreciation	
Light pink	Admiration, sympathy	
White	Reverence, humility	
Yellow	Joy, gladness	
Orange	Enthusiasm, desire	
Red and yellow	Gaiety, joviality	
Yellow	Sociability, friendship	

MY GOD

Do I Intentionally Embrace God's Special Instructions for Women?

10. Am I A Woman who says she is a Christian Or A Woman Who Is A Christian?

Ask yourself, 'Am I a woman who says she is a Christian or a woman who is a Christian?' On the surface, both parts of the question appear to be identical. However, a closer look reveals that the first part of the question describes a woman who desires all of the benefits of eternal life but daily chooses to embrace the philosophy of the world. Her daily choices, dress and speech reveal her allegiance just as Peter's speech betrayed him in the courtyard during Jesus' trial (Matt. 26:69-73).

The second portion of the question describes the woman who, by her lifestyle, clearly reflects that her values and character align with the Word of God. A woman who is a new creature (2 Cor. 5:17) in Christ chooses to …

∗ Love her Lord unreservedly (Mark 12:30).

∗ Regularly talk with her Lord through prayer and the reading of His Word (Phil. 4:6-7; 1 Thess. 5:17; Heb. 4:12).

∗ Believe that her heavenly Father will complete the good work He has begun in her (Phil. 1:6).

∗ Acknowledge that she can only complete her Father's work through His strength (Phil. 4:13).

∗ Seeks the Lord's wisdom rather than relying on her knowledge and experiences (James 1:5).

∗ Trusts that her Lord's ways are best (Prov. 3:5, 6).

As a woman seeking to acknowledge that God is your strength you will be careful to avoid the fatal errors of the woman who professes Christianity but whose character has not been renewed by the Word of God. Romans 12:1-2 clearly communicates that a Christian will daily manifest a renewed nature. This renewal comes from consistent study and meditation on Scripture (Ps. 119:11; Phil. 4:8-9; Col. 1:28, 3:10, 16). *God is My Strength* was written to assist you in this renewal process.

The lifestyle of the woman who is a Christian reflects her heavenly heritage and focuses on the development of what is truly permanent and noteworthy: her character. May I encourage you to consider the questions that follow to discern if you are a woman who says she is a Christian or a woman who is a Christian.

✳ Am I both a hearer and doer of biblical teaching? (James 1:22)

✳ Do I choose to model my life after the positive role models found in Scripture? (1 Cor. 10:11).

✳ Am I seeking to develop the gentle and quiet spirit that is precious to my heavenly Father? (1 Pet. 3:4)

✳ Am I a gracious woman even when others are not? (Prov. 11:16)

✳ Am I seeking to gain wisdom from God's Words so that I will be known as a wise woman? (Prov. 2:1-11)

Both the woman who says she is a Christian and the woman who is a Christian abide in the Christian community. However, only the woman who is a Christian will spend eternity with her heavenly Father (Rom. 3:10, 23; 5:8, 12; 6:23; 10:9, 10, 13). Are you a woman who says she is a Christian or a woman who is a Christian?

11. Have I Chosen to Embrace God's Special Instructions to Women?

If you embrace the popular teaching that God's special instructions to women are not relevant in the twenty-first century, then you do not believe in the immutability of God. God's word commands us to be 'doers of the word, and not merely hearers who deceive themselves' (James 1:22). When we search the Scriptures we uncover special instructions provided for us by Him; exploration of God's word reveals that a Christian woman is ...

✳ Aware that she was made by God in His own image (Gen. 1:27).

✳ A companion, helper and an equal to her husband[1] (Gen. 2:21-24).

✳ Gracious (Prov. 11:16).

✳ Discreet (Prov. 11:22).

✳ The crown of her husband (Prov. 12:4).

✳ Careful to build her house following the way of wisdom described in Prov. 9:1-6 (Prov. 14:1).

✳ The opposite of the contentious wife described throughout the book of *Proverbs* (Prov. 19:13; 21:9, 19; 25:24; 27:15-16).

✳ An asset to her husband (Prov. 18:22; 19:14).

✳ Worthy of praise (Ruth 3:11; Prov. 31:10-31).

✳ Cautious to avoid cultivating the behaviors associated with a seductress (Eccles. 7:26-28).

✳ Guarded in her behavior to prevent acquiring a reputation like the daughters of Zion (Isa. 3:16-24).

✳ Submissive to her husband (Eph. 5:22-23).

✳ Modest; her clothing reflecting that her heart is focused on God—especially for worship (1 Tim. 2:9).

✳ Trustworthy in all aspects of her life and ministry (1 Tim. 3:11).

✳ Willing to honor true widows (1 Tim. 5:1-16).

---

1. John MacArthur, *The MacArthur Study* Bible (Nashville: Word, 1997).

∗ Grounded in the Word of God (2 Tim. 3:6-7).

∗ Careful to develop a personal testimony that is consistent with her profession of faith (1 Tim. 2:10).

∗ Teachable (1 Tim. 2:11).

∗ Eager to train her children (2 Tim. 1:5).

∗ Available to teach the younger women (Titus 2:3-5).

∗ Excited about developing the type of character that pleases her heavenly Father (1 Pet. 3:1-6).

∗ Faithful to follow the examples of the women who walk through the pages of the Old and New Testament (1 Cor. 10:6; Heb. 11:11; 1 Pet. 3:1-6).

12. Do I View Myself as One of God's Precious Vessels?

What thoughts cross your mind when you read 1 Peter 3:7?

'You husbands in the same way, live with *your wives* in an understanding way, as with someone weaker, since she is a woman; and show her honor as a fellow heir of the grace of life, so that your prayers will not be hindered' (1 Pet. 3:7 NASB).

Do you view yourself as a precious *vessel* that your gracious heavenly Father designed for a specific purpose, or is your initial thought similar to one of my students? I can still visualize her reaction as I began reading this verse out loud in class. From the corner of my eye I observed her body language change dramatically after the phrase 'a weaker vessel' (1 Pet. 3:7 KJV). She was visibly displeased with the content. Knowing the student well, I was confident that as soon as we completed the reading she would have her hand raised—my intuition was correct.

Having taught for a number of years, I learned to pray and think on my feet. As I acknowledged the student I petitioned my heavenly Father for His response to her straightforward statement, 'I resent being labeled as weaker!' He graciously provided my response by 'fast forwarding' my eyes to the section of my notes that related to the verse, and I responded to her with these words …

'Peter provides a clear description of the attributes of godly living in the home and church in 1 Peter 3:1-12. He begins by describing the behavior that God expects of every wife in relationship to her husband (1 Pet. 3:1-6) and concludes with the relationship that should exist among Christians in general (1 Pet. 3:8-12).

'Sandwiched between the role of the wife and the relationship of Christians in general is a verse which provides the foundation for lasting harmony in the home—1 Peter 3:7. Three specific principles emerge from this verse:

✳ The husband is to live with the wife in an understanding way.

✳ The husband is to honor his wife.

✳ The husband and wife share a joint inheritance as 'heirs together of the grace of life.'

'The word *knowledge* is derived from the Greek word *gnosis*, which suggests that the knowledge is attained through study and practice—not simply a casual understanding. Peter's use of the word *likewise* links this instruction with the example of Christ's sacrificial and unjust suffering given in 1 Peter 2:21-25.

'Peter instructs the husband to honor his wife; this suggests that a woman is to be treated with esteem and dignity. *As unto the weaker vessel* does not suggest an inferior position, but rather one used for a special purpose. Fine china is not used for camping—not because it is inferior, but rather because it is designed for more elegant occasions. So the wife is not an inferior vessel, but rather one designed for a unique role.

'Peter's final instruction to husbands is a word of warning—recognize your wife as a fellow heir or your prayers will be hindered! Peter recognized that marriage is a reciprocal, not a one-sided, relationship. As husbands and wives acknowledge one another as *joint heirs together of the grace of life*, they will realize God's highest plan for their relationship.'

As I completed my brief summary her body language relaxed as she stated, 'Oh, that makes sense—I am not inferior, but simply designed for a different use.' I inwardly thanked my heavenly Father for His response.

Align your thoughts:

Consider your relationship with your heavenly Father: do you view yourself as a precious vessel He crafted for a unique purpose, or have you allowed the world's definition of a successful woman to blur the depth of His love for you? Today, spend time meditating on Jeremiah 31:3, Deuteronomy 7:6-8, Romans 5:6-11, 8:31-39, 2 Corinthians 4:7 and Ephesians 3:1-19 to establish in your mind the limitless, unconditional love your heavenly Father has for you—a love that is independent of how well you multi-task. Aligning your thoughts with His truth is the first step to acknowledging that you are indeed His precious *vessel*. This action continually provides you with strength for your daily journey!

13. How Can I Identify with the Woman Recorded in Proverbs 31?

Let me introduce you to the original busy woman—or woman of virtue. Her lifestyle, values and character align with the Word of God—and she is a woman whose life is as busy as we twenty-first century women are challenged to emulate. Why? Because the changelessness of God comes into question if Proverbs 31:10-31 is no longer relevant. If we believe God changed His mind about one passage of Scripture, how can we be sure He has not changed His mind about others?

God never changes. Nor do the principles He calls us to live by. Thus, the principles He gave for women in the Old and New Testaments still apply to women of the twenty-first century. We need to understand that the Proverbs 31 woman is not supposed to give us an inferiority complex. Rather, she provides a biblical foundation that enables today's woman to prioritize her life.

Eleven principles motivate the Godly Woman in Progress:

* she is virtuous (31:10)

* trustworthy (31:11-12)

* energetic (31:13-16, 19, 24, 27)

* physically fit (31:17)

* economical (31:18)

* unselfish (31:18)

* honorable (31:25)

* lovable (31:28-29)

* prepared (31:21-22)

* prudent (31:26)

* and God-fearing (31:30).

Proverbs 31:31 describes *the reward* of cultivating these eleven principles. When the busy woman seeks, through her heavenly Father's strength, to make them a part of her life, eventually she receives her rewards 'in the gates' (verse 31). This refers to the public assembly of people; such a woman is often rewarded in this life and will always be rewarded in eternity (1 Cor. 3:10-15; Rev. 22:12).

> *Finally, brothers and sisters, whatever is true, whatever is noble, whatever is right, whatever is pure, whatever is lovely, whatever is admirable—if anything is excellent or praiseworthy—think about such things. Whatever you have learned or received or heard from me, or seen in me—put it into practice. And the God of peace will be with you.*
> PHILIPPIANS 4:8-9

Moral purity, behaviors that model the Lord's character, and thoughts that are put through the filter of Philippians 4:8-9 describe how to put these principles into action. Moral purity means the busy woman chooses to avoid 'all appearance of evil' (1 Thess. 5:22). She will stop and think, *What would Jesus have me do?* before responding to any situation (1 Pet. 2:21-25). Philippians 4:8-9 filters her thoughts so that they are commendable, excellent and worthy of praise.

A goal most busy women desire to achieve is to positively influence their world. The eleven principles generate power and demand respect, thus allowing her to achieve that goal.

Align your thoughts

The Old Testament book of Ruth describes such a woman. Ruth 3:11 is the only scriptural reference to a *virtuous* woman and explains that Boaz knew of Ruth because of her reputation for purity. As others observe your life from a distance, as Boaz did Ruth's, would they describe you as *virtuous* woman? It is impossible for you to identify with the Proverbs 31 woman in your own strength. However, if you ask your heavenly Father to help you live a life characterized by Matthew 5:8, you will daily have the strength you need to do so.

> *Blessed are the pure in heart,*
> *for they will see God.*
> MATTHEW 5:8

Be sure to consistently look for evidence that He is saying 'yes' to your prayer, and thank Him for giving you the strength to pursue a *virtuous* lifestyle.

> *I can do all this through him*
> *who gives me strength.*
> PHILIPPIANS 4:13

14. Do My Daily Choices Reflect That I Walk Wisely?

Are you like the Proverbs 31 woman? Do you have a heart open to learning from the experience and wisdom of others?

Biblical wisdom is not just religious – it's practical too. When you fear and worship the Lord in His holiness this touches every area of life.

Take some time to read the following scriptures: Job 28:28; Psalm 111:10; Proverbs 1:7; 9:10.

Wisdom takes insights gleaned from the knowledge of God's Word and applies them to one's daily walk. We know the Scriptures provide the basis for possessing a teachable heart (Prov. 4:20-23), and we are reminded of Paul's teaching in 1 Corinthians 10:6 'now all these things became our examples, to the intent that we should not lust after evil things as they [the Israelites] also lusted.' Solomon's admonition to his son is a serious warning to us: '… fools despise wisdom and instruction' (Prov. 1:7). However, once we are convinced that we need to seriously consider the wisdom of mature saints, our next step in making sure that our lifestyle clearly demonstrates that our values and character align with the Word of God is to examine our daily walk. Let's pose a second probing question—do my daily choices reflect that I walk wisely? We will use an acrostic for the words *Walk Wisely* to answer this question …

W directs us to *wait* for the Lord rather than attempting to push our timetable (Psalm 37:34). Ask yourself, 'Am I like Ruth who chose to embrace Naomi's advice and wait for God's timing in her relationship with Boaz?' (Ruth 3:18)

A is a challenge to *abstain*. Simply stated, abstain tells us to stay away from anything that could possibly not be good for us. Read: 1 Thessalonians 5:22. This is a short but potent verse that basically says anything that is unbiblical should be shunned! Ask yourself, 'Do I abstain from *every* form of evil?'

L represents a word I hear often: *love*. If I am walking wisely I will choose to love the things God loves so that God, not the world, has the first place in my life (Matt. 10:32-39; Phil. 3:20). 1 John 2:17 reminds me that if I walk wisely I will abide with my heavenly Father forever. Ask yourself, 'Is my first love my heavenly Father or the things of the world?'

K focuses on knowledge. Proverbs 10:14 compels us to acquire biblical knowledge so that when we speak our words are filled with wisdom (Prov. 31:26). The loose tongue of fools is a recurring theme throughout Proverbs (10:6-8, 13, 18-19, 31-32; 12:23; 13:3; 15:1-2, 23, 26, 28, 31-33; 17:28; 18:2, 6-8) and is consistently repeated in the book of James (1:26; 3:1-12). Ask yourself, 'What is the source of my knowledge?'

W 'walking in the Spirit' (Gal. 5:16) provides us with the power to consistently make wise decisions. As we continue to obey the simple commands of Scripture we will mature in our decision-making process (Rom. 8:13; Eph. 5:15-17). A sobering question to ask is, 'Does my walk propel me away from fulfilling the lust of the flesh?'

I   spotlights *integrity*, a word that basically means that you choose to do what is right when given a choice between right and wrong. Psalm 15 describes the character of those who may dwell with the Lord and begins with integrity (Ps. 15:2). Is it a description of your character?

S   stands for the *Scriptures*, God's Word that has all of the answers to all of life's questions. However, they only answer the questions if we are using it as our primary resource (John 5:39). A study of Psalm 119 reveals all that God's Word will do for us—do we live like we believe it?

E   encourages us to endure when it is logical to quit. Romans 5:3 focuses on persevering under tremendous weight and pressure without succumbing (Rom. 15:5; Col. 1:22-23; 2 Thess. 1:4; Rev. 14:12). Though painful at times, the results reach into eternity. What does it take to stop me or make me give up?

L   motivates us to listen. Proverbs 19:20 directs us to listen to advice and accept instruction so that we will have the wisdom we need for the future. Proverbs 15:31 and James 1:19 focus on listening with a teachable spirit. Ask yourself, 'Am I quick to listen?'

Y   provides the final strategy in walking wisely, yielding to the Lord's direction in life. In the United States we have a very important traffic sign—it's an upside down triangle and is a clear warning that the other lane has the right of way. I must yield to the other traffic—or risk an accident! Refusing to yield may create unwanted challenges in my life. Equally important is the willingness for me to yield to my heavenly Father's specific instructions in relation to walking wisely; in reality I am demonstrating my love to Him by choosing to embrace these instructions with my whole heart—and that is when my joy is complete (1 John 1:4; 2 John 12). Am I quick to yield to my heavenly Father's instructions?

Align your thoughts

Are you willing to ask yourself at the beginning of each day, 'Will the choices that I make today reflect that I walk wisely?' Will you walk through the day using these questions as your road map so that at its conclusion your response is affirmative? If so, you are making wise choices!

15. Do My Life Choices Reflect My Royal Heritage?

When *Holiness, the Heart God Purifies* was released I was privileged to receive an inscribed copy from my friend, Nancy Leigh DeMoss. Having read the other two books in the trilogy, *Brokenness, the Heart God Revives* and *Surrender, the Heart God Controls*, I eagerly began to read the final volume. The introduction assured me that my life was going to be changed if I was going to do more than simply read the 194 pages. Nancy challenges her readers to expectantly pray the prayer below for a minimum of thirty days.

Oh, God,
Show me more of Your holiness.
Show me more of my sinfulness.
Help me to hate sin and to love righteousness as You do.
Grant me a deeper conviction of sin
And a more thorough spirit of repentance.
And make me holy as You are holy.[2]

I chose to accept the challenge and have actually continued to pray the prayer daily. Though radical changes did not occur over night I found that my appetite for activities I once enjoyed began to wane—they were not evil activities, but for me they were a hindrance to having a pure heart. As well, I realized that the more that I desired holiness the greater the likelihood that my life choices would reflect my royal heritage.

I would like to share with you some key meditation thoughts I developed that aid my application of this prayer. May I encourage you to meditate upon one a day, as well as to pray Nancy's prayer for a minimum of thirty days? If you will expectantly do so I believe that you will find, as I did, that your life choices will reflect your royal heritage.

Meditation Thoughts on My God

DAY ONE

God's Word says, 'Delight yourself also in the LORD, and He will give you the desires of your heart.' (Ps. 37:4 NKJV)

Therefore I may boldly say, 'The closer I draw to God, the more my desires will reflect His.'

2. Nancy Leigh DeMoss, *Holiness, the Heart God Purifies* (Chicago: Moody Publishers, 2004), 20.

DAY TWO

'The Lord thy God hath chosen you to be a people for his treasured possession …' (Deut. 7:6) Therefore I may boldly say, 'I am a treasured woman.'

DAY THREE

God has said, 'I have loved you with an everlasting love; therefore I have continued my faithfulness to you.' (Jer. 31:3)

Therefore I may boldly say, 'I am a deeply loved woman.'

DAY FOUR

God's Word says, 'All things work together for good to those who love me, and to those whom I have called.' (Rom. 8:28)

Therefore I may boldly say, 'God is aware of every situation I encounter and can fit it all into the master plan He has for my life.'

DAY FIVE

God's Word says, 'I can do all things through him who strengthens me.' (Phil. 4:13)

Therefore I may boldly say, 'Though I lack personal strength I can rest in the understanding that God will give me what I need.'

DAY SIX

God's Word says, 'Being confident of this very thing, that he which hath begun a good work in you will perform it until the day of Jesus Christ.' (Phil. 1:6)

Therefore I may boldly say, 'I am a woman in process.'

DAY SEVEN

God's Word says, 'Ye were not redeemed with perishable things …

But with the precious blood of Christ.' (1 Pet. 1:18-19)

Therefore I may boldly say, 'I am God's redeemed woman.'

DAY EIGHT

God's Word says, 'See what kind of love the Father has given to us that we should be called children of God …' (1 John 3:1)

Therefore I may boldly say, 'I am a woman of value.'

DAY NINE

God's Word says, 'I praise you; for I am fearfully and wonderfully made: wonderful are your works; my soul knows it very well.' (Ps. 139:14)

Therefore I may boldly say, 'I am a custom-made woman.'

DAY TEN

God has said, 'But let him who boasts boast in this, that he understands and knows me, that I am the Lord who practices steadfast love, justice and righteousness in the earth. For in these things I delight, declares the Lord.' (Jer. 9:24)

Therefore I may boldly say, 'I am a woman designed for a purpose.'

DAY ELEVEN

God has said, 'This people have I formed for myself; that they might declare my praise.' (Isa. 43:21)

Therefore I may boldly say, 'I am given an assignment.'

DAY TWELVE

God has said, 'Cast your burden upon the LORD, and he shall sustain you …' (Ps. 55:22 NASB)

Therefore I may boldly say, 'Though I have little strength of my own I am continually sustained by God's strength.'

DAY THIRTEEN

God has said, 'Do not be frightened, and do not be dismayed, for the Lord your God is with you wherever you go.' (Josh. 1:9)

Therefore I may boldly say, 'As God's woman I am always accompanied by Him.'

DAY FOURTEEN

Jesus says, 'You did not choose me, but I chose you, and appointed you that you should go and bear fruit and that your fruit should abide …' (John 15:16)

Therefore I may boldly say, 'I am God's responsibility.'

DAY FIFTEEN

God's Word says, 'Cast all your anxieties on him, because he cares for you.' (1 Pet. 5:7)

Therefore I may boldly say, 'I am under God's constant care.'

DAY SIXTEEN

Jesus says, 'Your Father knows what you need before you ask him.' (Matt. 6:8)

Therefore I may boldly say, 'The more I recognize my dependence on God, the more thankful I become, and the deeper my love for my Father grows.'

DAY SEVENTEEN

Jesus says, 'Peace I leave with you, my peace I give to you. Not as the world gives do I give to you. Let not your hearts be troubled, neither let them be afraid.' (John 14:27)

Therefore I may boldly say, 'Jesus' gift of peace offers me an alternative to fear and worry despite my circumstances.'

DAY EIGHTEEN

God's Word says, 'For though the LORD is high, he regards the lowly, but the haughty he knows from afar. Though I walk in the midst of trouble, you preserve my life; you stretch out your hand against the wrath of my enemies, and your right hand delivers me. The LORD will fulfill his purpose for me; your steadfast love, O LORD, endures forever. Do not forsake the work of your hands.' (Ps. 138:6-8)

Therefore I may boldly say, 'Though I can add effort to what God has given me to do, the basic building blocks are all courtesy of Him.'

DAY NINETEEN

God has said, 'I will give you a new heart and put a new spirit within you; I will take the heart of stone out of your flesh and give you a heart of flesh.' (Ezek. 36:26)

Therefore I may boldly say, 'Since God's spirit is resident in my life I can hear God's voice as He guides my decisions, sees me through *all* circumstances and fulfills His plans for me to become the woman He created me to be.'

DAY TWENTY

God's Word says, 'All have sinned and fall short of the glory of God, and are justified by his grace as a gift, through the redemption that is in Christ Jesus, whom God put forward as a propitiation by his blood to be received by faith. This was to show God's righteousness, because in his divine forbearance he had passed over former sins.' (Rom. 3:23-25)

Therefore I may boldly say, 'Because of Jesus, guilt and the fear of punishment no longer weigh me down. When I miss the mark I can seek God's forgiveness, learn from my mistakes, keep moving forward and forgive others just as I have been forgiven.'

DAY TWENTY ONE

God's Word says, 'And the word became flesh and dwelt among us, and we have seen his glory, glory as of the only Son from the Father, full of grace and truth.' (John 1:14)

Therefore I may boldly say, 'Jesus' humanity enabled Him to relate to my challenges, while His divinity gave Him the power to help me overcome them.'

DAY TWENTY TWO

Jesus has said, 'The thief comes only to steal and kill and destroy. I came that they might have life and have it more abundantly.' (John 10:10)

Therefore I may boldly say, 'Keeping in mind Jesus' promise to me of an abundant life gives me reason for constant hope and thanks. It also fosters contentment by helping me find joy in the abundance of what matters most.'

DAY TWENTY THREE

God's Word says, 'God is our refuge and strength, a very present help in trouble. Therefore we will not fear though the earth give way, though the mountains be moved into the heart of the sea, though its waters roar and foam, though the mountains tremble at its swelling.' (Ps. 46:1-3)

Therefore I may boldly say, 'God's answer to me when I am emotionally troubled is brief and straightforward: stop and remember who I am and that I am on your side.'

DAY TWENTY FOUR

God's Word says, 'Whatever you do, work heartily as for the Lord and not for men, knowing that from the Lord you will receive the inheritance as your reward. You are serving the Lord Christ.' (Col. 3:23-24)

Therefore I may boldly say, 'I am to focus on God's perspective through the day realizing it is Him that I am serving at home and at work rather than my husband, children or boss.'

DAY TWENTY FIVE

God's Word says, 'Now may the God of peace himself sanctify you completely and may your whole spirit and soul and body be kept blameless at the coming of our Lord Jesus Christ. He who calls you is faithful who will surely do it.' (1 Thess. 5:23-24)

Therefore I may boldly say, 'Paul's prayer should make me more aware of the big picture behind what is happening in my life. As I choose to keep God at the center of my life, I will find my own unique "picture" becoming more complete. My job, relationships and dreams work together, linked to one another because each should be solidly linked back to God.'

DAY TWENTY SIX

God's Word says, 'Be patient, therefore, brothers, until the coming of the Lord. See how the farmer waits for the precious fruit of the earth, being patient about it, until it receives the early and the late rains. You also, be patient. Establish your hearts, for the coming of the Lord is at hand. Do not grumble against one another, brothers, so that you may not be judged; behold, the Judge is standing at the door.' (James 5:7-9)

Therefore I may boldly say, 'I am to picture every prayer as a seed planted in God's will. As I wait, I should picture them ripening, trusting in God's perfect harvest time.'

DAY TWENTY SEVEN

God's Word says, 'Do not be anxious about anything but in everything by prayer and supplication with thanksgiving let your requests be made known to God. And the peace of God which surpasses all understanding, will guard your hearts and minds in Christ Jesus.' (Phil. 4:6-7)

Therefore I may boldly say, 'Peace and worry cannot coexist. Where worry is the potential enemy, peace is the faithful sentinel guarding my mind and heart. At the first sign of worry I am to practice the life-changing principle in Philippians 4:6-7 by thanking Him for who He is, for what He has done, and for the peace only He can provide.'

DAY TWENTY EIGHT

Jesus has said, 'Come to me, all who labor and are heavy laden, and I will give you rest. Take my yoke upon you, and learn from me, for I am gentle and lowly in heart, and you will find rest for your souls. For my yoke is easy, and my burden is light.' (Matt. 11:28-30)

Therefore I may boldly say, 'The rest Jesus offers is a quiet strength and companionship that helps me continue moving forward without burning out physically, mentally or emotionally.'

DAY TWENTY NINE

God's Word says, 'Blessed be the God and Father of our Lord Jesus Christ, the Father of mercies and God of all comfort, who comforts us in all our affliction, so that we may able to comfort those who are in any affliction, with the comfort with which we ourselves are comforted by God. For as we share abundantly in Christ's sufferings, so through Christ we share abundantly in comfort too.' (2 Cor. 1:3-5)

Therefore I may boldly say, 'As God comforts me I learn how to better comfort others even when I am busy.'

DAY THIRTY

God's Word says, 'For the LORD God is a sun and shield; the LORD bestows favor and honor. No good thing does he withhold from those who walk uprightly.' (Ps. 84:11)

Therefore I may boldly say, 'My job is to walk uprightly and believe that if my heavenly Father withholds something it is for my good.'

DAY THIRTY ONE

God's Word says, 'I can do all things through him who strengthens me.' (Phil. 4:13)

Therefore I may boldly say, 'Though I am weak through Christ I can complete the assignment *God* has given to me!'

So… The woman who trusts God as her strength …

* views herself as a precious vessel He crafted for a unique purpose (2 Cor. 4:7).

* has established in her mind the limitless, unconditional love her heavenly Father has for her (Jer. 31:3; Deut. 7:6-8; Rom. 5:6-11, 8:31-39; Eph. 3:1-19).

* makes cultivating a lifestyle that pleases her heavenly Father her top priority (Matt. 6:33).

* eagerly searches the Scriptures to discover His special instructions for her (John 5:39; Acts 17:11).

* eagerly embraces the biblical standards for the role of women (Prov. 31:30; 1 Pet. 3:4).

* believes that God's instructions will make her happy, as she chooses to trust her heavenly Father that there is no good thing He will withhold from her if she is walking uprightly (Ps. 84:11).

* desires to be both theologically sound and practically adept, thus choosing to prove herself a doer of the word, and not merely a hearer who deceives herself (James 1:22).

* identifies the 'high places' in her life; seeks, through her Lord's strength, to 'utterly destroy them' (Deut. 12:1-7).

* acknowledges that the woman described in Proverbs 31 is a woman whose life twenty-first century Christian women are challenged to emulate (Prov. 31:10-31).

* lives in such a way that Jesus' words in Matthew 25:21 characterize her daily life.

* purposes to skillfully apply biblical truth to practical living (James 4:17).

* intentionally makes choices that reflect her royal heritage (Lev. 20:7; 1 Thess. 5:23-24).

Building My Spiritual Stamina

*Continually think about or contemplate the Scriptures
that focus your mind on qualities that promote a healthy
relationship with your heavenly Father (cf. PHIL. 4:8)*

*Consecrate yourself, therefore, and be holy,
for I am the LORD your God.*
LEVITICUS 20:7

*For you are a people holy to the LORD your God. The LORD
your God has chosen you to be a people for his treasured
possession, out of all the peoples who
are on the face of the earth.*
DEUTERONOMY 7:6

*The LORD appeared to him from far away.
I have loved you with an everlasting love;
therefore, I have continued my faithfulness to you.*
JEREMIAH 31:3

*The fear of the LORD is the beginning of knowledge;
fools despise wisdom and instruction.*
PROVERBS 1:7

*Charm is deceitful, and beauty is vain,
but a woman who fears the LORD is to be praised.*
PROVERBS 31:30

*And you shall love the Lord your God with all your heart
and with all your soul and with all your mind.*
MARK 12:30

57

For while we were still weak, at the right time
Christ died for the ungodly.
ROMANS 5:6

What then shall we say to these things?
If God is for us, who can be against us?
ROMANS 8:31

But we have this treasure in jars of clay,
to show that the surpassing power of God
belongs to God and not to us.
2 CORINTHIANS 4:7

Now may the God of peace himself
sanctify you completely,
And may your whole spirit and soul and
body be kept blameless at the coming of
our Lord Jesus Christ.
He who calls you is faithful; he will surely do it.
1 THESSALONIANS 5:23-24

Sustaining My Spiritual Stamina

Further study to encourage renewal of your
mind and spirit (cf. EPH. 4:17-32)

✳ Search each of the verses listed in the chart below. Read them
in the context of the Bible chapter in which they were written.
Personalize your search by completing the right hand column
of the chart.

GOD'S SPECIAL INSTRUCTIONS TO [YOUR NAME]
A GODLY WOMAN IN PROGRESS

Verse(s)	Instruction	Personal Application
Genesis 1:27	Aware that she was made by God in His own image.	
Genesis 2:18, 21-24	A companion, helper and an equal to her husband.	
Proverbs 11:16	Gracious.	
Proverbs 11:22	Discreet.	
Proverbs 12:4	The crown of her husband.	
Proverbs 14:1	Careful to build her house following the way of wisdom described in Proverbs 9:1-6.	
Proverbs 18:22; 19:14	An asset to her husband.	
Proverbs 19:13; 21:9, 19; 27:15-16	The opposite of the contentious wife described throughout the book of *Proverbs*.	
Ruth 3:11, Proverbs 31:10-31	Virtuous.	
Ecclesiastes 7:26-28	Cautious to not cultivate the behaviors of a seductress.	
Isaiah 3:16-24	Guarded in her behavior so she does not gain the reputation of the daughters of Zion.	

GOD'S SPECIAL INSTRUCTIONS TO [YOUR NAME]
A GODLY WOMAN IN PROGRESS

Verse(s)	Instruction	Personal Application
Ephesians 5:22-23	Submissive to her husband.	
1 Timothy 2:9	Modest; her clothing reflecting that her heart is focused on God— especially for worship.	
1 Timothy 2:10	Careful to develop a personal testimony consistent with her profession of faith.	
1 Timothy 2:11	Teachable.	
1 Timothy 3:11	Trustworthy in all aspects of her life and ministry.	
1 Timothy 5:1-16	Willing to honor true widows.	
2 Timothy 1:5	Eager to train her children.	
2 Timothy 3:6-7	Grounded in the Word of God.	
Titus 2:3-5	Available to learn from an older woman or to teach the younger women.	
1 Peter 3:1-6	Excited about developing the type of character that pleases her heavenly Father.	

* Research the eleven principles that motivate the Godly Woman in Proverbs—virtuous (31:10), trustworthy (31:11-12), energetic (31:13-16, 19, 24, 27), physically fit (31:17), economical (31:18), unselfish (31:18), honorable (31:25), lovable (31:28-29), prepared (31:21-22), prudent (31:26) and God-fearing (31:30).

[YOUR NAME] A GODLY WOMAN IN PROGRESS		
Principle ... defined in your words	Scripture Reference	Personal Application
Virtuous		
Trustworthy		
Energetic		
Physically Fit		
Economical		
Unselfish		
Honorable		
Lovable		
Prepared		
Prudent		
God-Fearing		

* Study the lives of each of the women presented in the Old and New Testaments. Purpose to learn from their examples by completing the following chart:

GOD'S SPECIAL INSTRUCTIONS TO [YOUR NAME] A GODLY WOMAN IN PROGRESS		
Woman	Scripture Reference	Personal Application
Sarah		
Rahab		
Ruth		
Naomi		
Esther		
Mary		
Anna		
Elizabeth		
Eunice		

✳ Using the Scriptures presented in this chapter and supported by your own Scripture search, formulate a **Life Mission Statement** that reflects your understanding of God's Special Instructions to Women.

Just to get you started, my **Life Mission Statement** is to:

➥ Love my Lord with all my heart (Mark 12:30).

➥ Walk worthy of my profession (Eph. 4:1-3).

➥ Train the younger women (Titus 2:3-5).

MYSELF

Am I Preserving the Temple of the Holy Spirit?

16. What is the Heart?

When the word *heart* is mentioned, what thoughts fill your mind? Valentine cards with lace and flowers, a doctor's appointment for an electrocardiograph (ECG), or perhaps an evaluation of your own heart in light of the Scriptures? As Christian women we should be concerned with two forms of our hearts: our physical heart and our spiritual heart.

The physical heart provides nourishment, sustenance and energy throughout the entire body. If a weakness, either by breakdown or disease, occurs within the heart, it could lead to weaknesses in the rest of the body. The spiritual heart is the center of thinking and reason (Prov. 3:3, 6:21, 7:3), the emotions (Prov. 15:15, 30) and the will (Prov. 11:20). It is the source of whatever affects our speech (Prov. 4:24), sight (Prov. 4:25) and conduct (Prov. 4:26-27). The condition of our spiritual heart determines our spiritual health and ultimately controls how we respond to life's circumstances.

Proverbs teaches us that we have either a wicked and foolish heart or a righteous and wise heart. The wicked and foolish heart despises correction (Prov. 5:12), is proud (Prov. 10:14, 18:2, 12), lacks discretion (Prov. 12:23, 19:3) and is hard (Prov. 28:14). Standing in stark contrast is the righteous and wise heart that receives commands (Prov. 10:8), has wisdom and understanding (Prov. 14:33), seeks knowledge (Prov. 15:14), and learns and grows (Prov. 16:23). As a Godly Woman in Progress are you choosing to keep your heart with all vigilance, realizing that from it flows the springs of life (Prov. 4:23)? Strategies to do so include …

∗ knowing how to guard against a spiritual heart attack.

∗ choosing to speak graciously.

∗ cultivating a grateful spirit.

∗ forgiving others.

∗ winning over worry.

∗ dealing actively with discouragement.

∗ facing fear head on.

∗ viewing your worth through the lens of Scripture.

∗ selecting garments that reflect your royal heritage.

Let's consider each strategy in the questions that follow!

17. Do I Know How to Guard Against a Spiritual Heart Attack?

Are you as careful with your spiritual health as your physical health? I am sure that you know that good physical health is the result of implementing sound health practices just as good spiritual health is the outcome of developing sound spiritual practices. When we undergo a medical examination four vital statistics are normally discussed: our blood pressure, pulse, weight and diet. Did you know our heavenly Father's spiritual health examination for a Godly Woman in Progress contains the same four essential statistics? Consider this comparison …

MEDICAL EXAMINATION	SPIRITUAL HEALTH EXAMINATION
Blood pressure	Our reading of anxiety over trust (Ps. 55:22)
Pulse	The rhythm of our gratitude (Col. 3:12-17)
Weight	Our need to eliminate unneeded cares (1 Pet. 5: 6-10)
Diet	A regular intake and submission to the life-giving thoughts of the Lord (Jer. 15:16)

The choice to embrace sound spiritual practices allows a woman who acknowledges that God is her strength to mature in a number of godly character qualities including:

✳ Submission to her Lord (Col. 3:18).

✳ Submission to the authority figures in her life (Col. 3:22-24; Eph. 5:22).

65

* Respect for her husband (1 Pet. 3:1-6).

* Commitment to loving her family (Titus 2:4).

* Faithfulness as a friend (Prov. 17:17).

* Compassion for those in need (Prov. 31:20).

* Care of her household (Titus 2:5).

* Self-control, kindness, and purity of heart and mind (Titus 2:5).

* Maintenance of her body as a precious vessel on loan to her from her heavenly Father (1 Cor. 6:19-20).

The consistent development of these godly qualities generally produces a heart of contentment—one of the best health practices that prevents a spiritual heart attack and demonstrates to the world that God is our strength. Let's take a moment to diagnose our level of contentment …

* Do others affirm my character (am I worth more than fine jewels)? (Prov. 31:10)

* Do I gain the confidence of my husband or others who consistently observe my actions? (Prov. 31:11)

* Do I approach my work eagerly and vigorously? (Prov. 31:14,17)

* Am I hospitable to my children and others? (Prov. 31:15)

* Do I practice sound money management? (Prov. 31:16, 18, 24)

* Am I willing to share my goods with those who are needy? (Prov. 31:20)

* Do I prepare ahead of time for my family's needs? (Prov. 31:21)

* Am I confident and dignified? (Prov. 31:25)

* Am I a wise and good teacher? (Prov. 31:26)

* Do I willingly oversee the activities of my household? (Prov. 31:27)

* Have I earned the respect of my family? (Prov. 31:28)

* Do I fear the Lord? (Prov. 31:30)

Well, what was your diagnosis? Are you in good spiritual health, or are you dangerously close to a spiritual heart attack? What are the areas that could stand some improvement? Perhaps one is forgiveness, which forms the basis of our next question.

18. Is My Reflex Reaction to Choose Forgiveness?

Aunt Joan isn't attending the family reunion this summer because last year she was offended by a remark John made about her 'famous deviled eggs'. After moving to her son-in-law and daughter's home and funding the construction of her own granny flat, Ellen moved out four years later. The root cause of both scenarios? The failure to forgive.

Read: Matthew 18:21-35 and Luke 17:3-4.

Much like the legendary *Spanish Water Torture* where victims were strapped down so they could not move, and cold water was dripped slowly on to a small area of the body until they were gradually driven frantic, so the choice to withhold forgiveness slowly but effectively destroys family unity. The antidote? Follow our Lord's example and develop a *forgiving spirit*.

> *For you have been called for this purpose, since Christ also suffered for you, leaving you an example for you to follow in His steps,* WHO COMMITTED NO SIN, NOR WAS ANY DECEIT FOUND IN HIS MOUTH; *and while being reviled, He did not revile in return; while suffering, He uttered no threats, but kept entrusting Himself to Him who judges righteously.*
>
> 1 PETER 2:21-23 NASB

Forgiveness is the foundation of all relationships. Though the actions of others will at times disappoint us, from a biblical perspective we are to forgive them unconditionally. It is a sobering thought to realize that relationships fracture if we refuse to forgive.

When our sinful reactions collide with another's, anger often results. Anger breeds an unforgiving spirit and damages relationships. To avoid that heartache, Ephesians 4:26 calls us to deal with broken relationships before we lay our heads on the pillow at night.

Matthew 5:43-48 teaches that to forgive is the most God-like action possible. God by nature is a forgiving God. We reflect His character when we choose to forgive (Eph. 4:32; 1 John 1:9). Peter generously offered to forgive seven times. Jesus corrected his faulty reasoning by suggesting that he was to forgive at least 490 times!

Matthew 18:21-35 clearly teaches that those forgiven the greater sins are to forgive the lesser sins. We practice the truth of these when we offer the same mercy to others that God daily extends to us. Holding a grudge is an unrighteous act. Eventually it will produce a bitter spirit. How many times are we to forgive others? The same number of times we are forgiven—a number that far exceeds 490!

Failure to forgive can impact fellowship with others. Consider again Matthew 18:21-35. The other servants observed the lack of compassion the forgiven servant demonstrated toward his debtor. They reported this behavior to their Master. The result of his unforgiving spirit created a greater debt than what was originally forgiven.

As well, failure to forgive eventually results in serious spiritual consequences, such as divine chastening (Matt. 18:32-35; James 2:13) and an estranged relationship with our heavenly Father (Matt. 6:12-15).

So, how do we model Christ's example and develop a *forgiving spirit?* Nurture the essential character qualities of kindness, compassion, humbleness, meekness, patience and tolerance with others (Col. 3:12-13). Deliberately choose to forgive and forget unkind deeds. Release the grudges we hold against others. This is essential (Ps. 103:12; Heb. 10:18). Such actions contribute to family unity and exemplify Christ's sacrifice for us. As Jesus was dying upon the cross, He prayed, 'Father, forgive them, for they do not know what they are doing' (Luke 23:34). Regardless of the offense against us, Christ's response compels us to follow His example. The following *Principles* provide the foundation for developing a *forgiving spirit.*

Forgiveness Principles

* God forgave us first. Follow His example and forgive others (Matt. 6:12; Luke 11:4; Eph. 4:31-32).

* Forgive from the heart and work toward reconciliation whenever possible (Matt. 5:23-24).

✳ Do not seek revenge. That it is not God's plan for believers. He reserves that for Himself (Heb. 10:30).

✳ Forgive as God has commanded believers. Failure to do so is an act of direct disobedience against Him (Luke 17:3-4).

✳ Assume personal responsibility for your part in relational collisions (James 5:16).

✳ Acknowledge that holding a grudge hinders your walk with the Lord (Mark 11:25; Eph. 4:32).

Align your thoughts

All the injuries and injustices that others commit against us are the trials God uses to perfect us. Realign reactions to them and view them as tools by which our heavenly Father makes us more like Christ, as this is a godly response (James 1:2; 1 Pet. 5:10; 2 Cor. 12:7). When we respond to trials biblically our spiritual stamina increases because God's strength is perfected in *our* weakness. Can you imagine the outcome had Aunt Joan and Ellen viewed their situations through this perspective?

19. Don't All Women Have Tongue Issues?

How beautiful is your tongue—or have you never really considered your tongue in terms of its attractiveness? You normally don't check it in the mirror multiple times during the day, go on shopping trips for it, schedule appointments for it at the tongue beautician, or purchase cosmetics for it. Yet it is the tongue, more than the shape of your face or the dimensions of your figure or your theological knowledge, which determines your beauty.

Physically, the tongue is one of the body's most versatile organs. It plays an important role in speaking and in eating. It is also the bearer of taste and tactile sensations and so gives you pleasure in eating. It gives warning of possible injury by registering pain when foods are too hot and revulsion when they are spoiled. In its role as manipulator, the tongue takes food into the mouth, moves it between the upper and lower teeth for chewing, and then molds the crushed and moistened particles into a ball for swallowing.

Spiritually, James 3:3-5 teaches that even though the tongue is small, it has the power to control a person and everything in their life. Isaiah 6:1-8 relates the account of how God called Isaiah to become a prophet. He did so by first giving Isaiah a vision of His awesome holiness and then by sanctifying the prophet's lips. Isaiah realized, after catching a glimpse of the purity of God, that his lips needed to be purified (6:5-8).

James 3:8 reminds us that no man, only God by His power, can tame or beautify the tongue—thus our need to schedule an appointment at God's Tongue Toning Spa to maintain a beautiful tongue. Let's begin our appointment by completing the brief beauty consultation for your tongue.

A BEAUTY CONSULTATION FOR MY TONGUE

Place the number that best reflects your response to the statement in the space provided.*

1. I have a challenge controlling my tongue:
   5 = never; 4 = very seldom; 3 = seldom;
   2 = sometimes; 1 = usually; 0 = regularly.

2. After an argument, I usually feel that I was most hurt by:
    2 = the issues that were involved;
    1 = the words that were said.

3. In relation to gossip, I feel that I am guilty of this:
    4 = never; 3 = seldom; 2 = sometimes;
    1 = frequently.

4. During this past week I chose to use my tongue constructively to:
    5 = comfort a friend; 4 = express love to my parents;
    3 = encourage someone in leadership;
    2 = express sympathy or concern;
    1 = witness for Christ.

5. Generally, I believe I talk:
    3 = the right amount; 2 = too little; 1 = too much.

6. The misuses of the tongue I have under control include:
    7 = too talkative; 6 = complaining; 5 = gossiping;
    4 = lying; 3 = exaggerating; 2 = boastful;
    1 = too loud.

7. The qualities of the biblical use of the tongue that I have cultivated are:
    3 = kind; 2 = affirming; 1 = contented.

8. I have an appreciative tongue:
    4 = frequently; 3 = sometimes; 2 = seldom;
    1 = never.

9. I practice the Ecclesiastes 'a time to' passage and know when to keep silent and when to speak:
   4 = frequently; 3 = sometimes; 2 = seldom;
   1 = never.

10. I am prone to nagging:
    4 = never; 3 = seldom; 2 = sometimes;
    1 = frequently.

.... **Consultation Total**

*Your number is the sum of all of the items that apply to you. An interpretation of your consultation is found at the conclusion of the question.

When we begin an exercise program, a set of baseline measurements is helpful. The same is true with Tongue Toning. Let's collect some baseline measurements by completing the chart below.

TONGUE TONING BASELINE CHART	
CATEGORY	MEASUREMENT
Approximate length of my tongue	
My height in inches	
Percentage of my height that is tongue: Tongue length divided by Height = ... or .... % My tongue length is 2.5" and my height is height is 66" $\frac{2.5}{66}$ = .03 or 3%	

Having completed the baseline measurements, respond to this single evaluation question: Am I going to allow something that is .... % (insert your calculation) of my body height to control me?

Now you need to organize your Tongue Toning regimen. You may choose from the following options:

Be Appreciative

A sign of genuine godliness is a sincere display of appreciation before your heavenly Father. What is the tragic fault of those who have drifted away from God? Read Romans 1:21-27. The root cause was thanklessness. Those with beautiful tongues consistently express appreciation to their heavenly Father and others.

Be Quiet

This is difficult to implement because it takes more muscle power to keep the tongue silent than to activate it. James 1:19 challenges us to be 'slow to speak'. You can often be a great help to others by simply listening.

Be Affirming

The act of affirmation inspires others with renewed courage, spirit and hope. It affirms individuals for who they are rather than for what they do. Proverbs 25:11 teaches us the value of affirming words: '*a word fitly spoken is like apples of gold in a setting of silver.*'

Be Contented

A grumbling, complaining tongue is an ugly tongue, while a contented tongue is a beautiful tongue. Going through life with a complaining spirit is like driving a car with your eye constantly on the rear-view mirror. Philippians 2:14-15 teaches us that we are to '*do all things without grumbling or disputing …*' Instead of complaining about what you don't have, practice the truth of Philippians 3:13-14 and press forward to what lies ahead.

At the end of the age we will be judged by how we have used our tongues. Matthew 12:36 teaches that '*for every idle word men may speak, they will give account of it in the day of judgment.*' What type of Tongue Toning Regimen will make your tongue a beautiful tongue?

Beauty Consultation for My Tongue Interpretation

41-37   A maturing, appreciative, quiet, affirming, contented tongue

36-33   A commitment to an appreciative, quiet, affirming, contented tongue

32-29   An understanding of what constitutes an appreciative, quiet, affirming, contented tongue

28-25   A minimal commitment to an appreciative, quiet, affirming, contented tongue

24- 0   A tongue transplant is needed

20. How Can I Cope with Loneliness?

The radiant smile Ashley spontaneously flashes and her effervescent personality are a mask she dons each day when she leaves her apartment. Inwardly an empty hole rests in the place where her heart once resided. The reason? She believes that no one really cares about her as a person. If she was suddenly hospitalized there would be no cards, flowers or visitors. Ashley's radiant smile and effervescent personality are simply a coping technique for dealing with the loneliness that shrouds her life. Ashley is a silent sufferer because she lacks the biblical resources that allow her to be a victor rather than a victim when she is attacked by the loneliness epidemic.

The Loneliness Epidemic

Half a century ago, Yale University Press published the first edition of *The Lonely Crowd* by David Riesman with Nathan Glazer and Reuel Denney.[1] Though the contents of the book do not teach the reader how to deal with loneliness, its title is a reminder that loneliness is a common epidemic. It is not limited to the person who lives alone, who is confined to a nursing home and is rarely visited, or even the truck driver who spends much time on the road alone. Regrettably, the loneliness epidemic attacks the Christian community as frequently as secular society.

If we are honest, most of us long for the kind of 'kindred spirit' friend so eloquently described by Anne Shirley in the classic story of an orphan girl, *Anne of Green Gables*.[2] Her longing is replicated in the hearts of people everywhere because, as Ecclesiastes 4:9-12 teaches, we all have a built-in need for companionship.

Numerous research studies reinforce what Anne Shirley and Solomon, the author of Ecclesiastes 4:9-12, taught

---

1. http://www.nytimes.com/books/00/01/09/bookend/bookend. html
2. Lucy Maud Montgomery, *Anne of Green Gables* (New York: Grosset and Dunlap, 1935).

centuries ago. 'Two are better than one because they have a good reward for their toil. For if they fall, one will lift up his fellow. But woe to him who is alone when he falls and has not another to lift him up!' Take, for example, the research conducted by the University of Chicago. Its findings report that loneliness undermines health as well as mental well-being. The impact of loneliness is so detrimental that chronic loneliness belongs among such health risk factors as smoking, obesity or lack of exercise. The studies, reported in a book entitled *Loneliness: Human Nature and the Need for Social Connection*, show that a sense of rejection or isolation disrupts not only abilities, will power and perseverance, but also key cellular processes deep within the human body.[3]

What Is Loneliness?
The definition of loneliness varies from individual to individual. For me it is a painful awareness that I was excluded from a meaningful event. Like Ashley, when I experience loneliness I feel that no one cares about me. When the loneliness epidemic strikes, even the things I enjoy the most seem pointless because, when I reach out to share them with others, there is no one there to respond. If I choose to allow my thoughts to continue in a downward spiral I will quickly lose my spiritual vitality.

When defining loneliness I must be careful to not confuse it with solitude. When I choose to purposely withdraw myself from others for a period of time I experience solitude. It is a time when I want or need to be alone. Jesus modeled

3. http://www.physorg.com/

the need for solitude in Matthew 14:23. Loneliness, on the other hand, is the painful experience of wanting to be with others but being excluded. It feels like a dull aching pain which no doctor's prescription can alleviate.

Often loneliness does not come because of the absence of people around us. Sometimes a large gathering is a very lonely place. Loneliness is not dependent upon the number of people with whom you may be, but rather on your relationship to those people. You can be utterly desolate and lonely in a crowd or delivered completely from all loneliness with one person. The number of people is not relevant. The relationship with the person or people is.

So is there a cure for Ashley's loneliness? Absolutely! Since she is God's child He promises to provide her with a permanent cure—and He is willing to do the same for all who are willing to follow His prescription!

God's Cure for the Loneliness Epidemic

Some people learn to enjoy the self-pity and pain that emanate from the loneliness epidemic and are unwilling to do anything to change their situation. But, if you are seriously interested in doing something about your loneliness, there are steps you can take to cure the epidemic. Consider taking this following prescription when the epidemic threatens to strike:

✳ Practice the truth of Proverbs 18:24 and become a bridge-builder. Many people experience loneliness because they are waiting for someone to build a bridge to them. Invite, visit, call or e-mail several people. Focus on building relationships with others rather than waiting for someone to build a bridge to you.

✳ Purpose to become a blessing to others. Rather than drowning in self-pity remember that as God's child you were redeemed to glorify Him. 1 Corinthians 10:31 reminds us that whatever we do we are to do it to the glory of God. Consider how you might be a blessing to others. For example, pray about and investigate the possibility of becoming involved in meaningful community and church projects. Consider visiting those whom you know to be in more challenging conditions than you are. Convalescent facilities, homes for the aged and hospitals are always in need of individuals to share a word of cheer or offer a helping hand.

✳ Put into practice Hebrews 13:5 and focus on the truth that though human relationships may fail you, God promises to *never* leave nor forsake you. Cultivate an ongoing, vital relationship with your heavenly Father. Then, when there is no human to encourage or affirm you, your relationship with your heavenly Father will prevent loneliness and its buddy depression from submerging you in self-pity.

✳ Ponder the reality that loneliness is curable. Numerous scripture passages outline the treatment for replacing loneliness with spiritual vitality.

> ➤ Begin by acknowledging that everyone experiences pockets of loneliness in their lives. Turn them into solitude retreats and savor the exclusive time with your heavenly Father.

> ➤ Maintain sound nutritional habits. Inadequate nutrition may prolong the loneliness epidemic.

> ➤ Be spiritually prepared. Similar to saving a percentage of each check for unforeseen expenses, build a spiritual reserve for pockets of loneliness. If you consistently internalize God's Word (Ps. 119:11), you will possess

spiritual vitality (Ps. 1:2). This internalization process begins with spending time daily reading and thinking about the Scriptures, asking your heavenly Father how you should apply them to everyday life, purposing to be obedient through His strength, and joyfully responding to His instructions (Phil. 4:13).

➤ Seek to apply the truth of Jeremiah 17:7-8. Acknowledge that the heat will come; the drought is certain; however, there is a supernatural source of vitality when one is spiritually prepared.

If you consistently follow this treatment you should possess a more finely-toned spiritual constitution that allows you to say, 'I am a loneliness epidemic survivor and now possess spiritual **VITALITY** because I chose to:

✳ be a Victor rather than a victim (Rom. 8:26-39),

✳ walk in Integrity (Ps. 15),

✳ Trust in the Lord (Prov. 3:5-6),

✳ Abide in Christ (John 15:1-11),

✳ Love my Lord with all my heart (Matt. 22:34-39),

✳ Incline my heart to my heavenly Father's testimonies (Ps. 119:36),

✳ Thank my heavenly Father for the benefits of being His child (Ps. 103),

✳ Yield myself to the Lord (2 Chron. 30:8).'

Align Your Thoughts:

The choice is yours. Will you choose to silently suffer like Ashley or will you eagerly follow the treatment that allows you to be a victor rather than a victim when you are attacked by the loneliness epidemic?

21. Is It Possible to be Single and Satisfied?

As a Christian woman, trained as a Home Economist, I never expected to be single past my mid-twenties. However, the Lord had a much different plan for me and has gently matured my attitude toward singleness, as well as the purpose of marriage. Rather than marriage only providing an intimate, nurturing relationship, I know now that I should marry only if our united lives would be more effective for the Lord than either of us in our single state.

As a single professional I established Home Economics Departments in three Christian colleges and one seminary. I daily experience the joy of watching numerous young women mature into useful instruments for our Master's Kingdom. Though I have no children of my own, I have spiritual children and grandchildren all over the world. My single status allows me to provide the nurturing that my students need without neglecting my own family. I consistently have the joy of experiencing what Paul wrote about in 1 Corinthians 7:32-34!

> *But I want you to be free from concern. One who is unmarried is concerned about the things of the Lord, how he may please the Lord; but one who is married is concerned about the things of the world, how he may please his wife, and his interests are divided. The woman who is unmarried, and the virgin, is concerned about*

*the things of the Lord, that she may be holy both in body
and spirit; but one who is married is concerned about the
things of the world, how she may please her husband.*

1 Corinthians 7:32-34 nasb

My greatest challenge in experiencing contentment in my
single state is members of the Body of Christ! Yes – there are
those who just cannot understand how someone who can
cook and sew, as well as implement effective management
and financial skills, is not married. Their insistence that 'Mr
Right' will one day come along discounts the possibility
that it is the Lord's will for me to minister to others as
a single, using my spiritual gifts, talents and educational
background.

Can Any Good Thing Result from Remaining Single?
Current statistics remind us that 99.6 million Americans 18
and older in 2010 were unmarried. This group comprised
43.6 percent of the population.[4] The statistic suggests that
a percentage of Christian men and women will not marry.
Paul addresses the practical advantages of singleness.

Read: 1 Corinthians 7:7-9 and 7:25-40.

A primary reason for remaining single, according to
Paul, is the special freedom and independence afforded to
the individual. Precious in the sight of God are the men
and woman who use their days of singleness to concentrate
on becoming complete in Christ and tending to their

---

4. America's Families and Living Arrangements: 2010 http://www.
census.gov/population/www/socdemo/hh-fam/cps2010.html;
Tables A1 and A2

Father's affairs (Luke 2:49). As well, it is important that the Christian community encourages singles toward spiritual maturity so that they are prepared for the heavenly Father's next assignment (Jer. 29:11-13). Spiritual maturity for the single saint includes growing in their personal character (1 Pet. 2:21-3:22), understanding God's purpose for the home (Gen. 2:21-24), developing a heart of contentment (John 14:1-3), learning how to effectively manage their *current* home (Prov. 24:3), growing in graciousness (Prov. 11:16; 2 Pet. 3:18), practicing biblical stewardship (Matt. 25:21), implementing hospitality (Rom. 12:13), broadening their world view (Matt. 5:13-16), understanding the contribution they can *currently* make to the Body of Christ (Rom.12:4-6) and ensuring that God's Word is not discredited.

Read: Titus 2:1-15

The table found at the conclusion of this question offers some suggestions for the entire Body of Christ to assist the single saint in achieving their completeness in Christ (Col. 3:10).

A Critical Choice

The wise single's choice to become complete in Christ eliminates the need of looking to other people and other situations to meet their needs. Only spiritual maturity, not professional achievement, marriage, children or ministry success will stimulate spiritual completeness to flourish in their lives. Several concepts of completeness emerge as the single saint views singleness from eternity's perspective:

✳ their growth commences by 'holding fast' to Christ (John 17:3; Eph. 2:1-10; Col. 2:19; 1 Pet. 1:23).

* they are capable of doing what God has called them to do (2 Tim. 3:17).

* they acknowledge Christ as their authoritative Head (Eph. 1:22-23).

* their strength to deal with Satan's temptations develops as they mature in Christ (Eph. 6:10-20; 1 Pet. 5:7-9).

* their value system is in the proper perspective (Matt. 6:19-21, 33; Col. 2:20-23).

* they recognize they are equipped to become involved in the work of the ministry (1 Cor. 12:12-31; Eph. 4:7-16).

* their completeness in Christ and effective ministry occur only with the combination of Divine Assistance and Personal Responsibility (Phil. 4:13)!

* they acknowledge that dying to self and the world is a part of the process (Gal. 2:20; Col. 2:20; 1 Pet. 1:2-4).

* know, through their knowledge of God, that God does not complete those who put him in second place (Deut. 10:12-13, 30:6; Matt. 22:37-39; Mark 12:29-31).

* they acquire a humble faith as the process is carried to completion (Col. 3:9-12).

* they are confident that as they walk uprightly there is no good thing that their heavenly Father will withhold from them (Ps. 84:11).

Realigning Your Focus

Those who view singleness from eternity's perspective focus on their heavenly Father. The more they realign their focus the more they demonstrate their love toward Him (1 John 2:3-6). The world says others' affirmation of them confirm or negate their value as a person. God's Word states that as His son or daughter, they are loved even when no human affirms them (Jer. 31:3). A number of biblical references affirm that singles are loved …

* they are God's special treasure … chosen by Him (Exod. 19:5; 1 Pet. 2:9).

* they were created in the image of God (Gen. 1:27).

* they were created for His glory (Isa. 43:7).

* He keeps them as the 'apple of His eye' (Deut. 32:10).

* their loving heavenly Father created them, formed them, redeemed them, called them by name and claims them as His very own (Isa. 43:1).

* when they were at their worst God gave, out of a heart of love, His very best for them (Rom. 5:8).

Contentment is a Choice

The single saint understands that marriage is not a condition for salvation, a command or the standard for everyone. Reflecting on 1 Corinthians 7:17-24, they are encouraged to be content with their marital status and wholeheartedly serve their Lord rather than living in a state of limbo until 'Mr or Miss Right' appears (1 Cor. 7:32; Phil. 4:11; Heb. 13:5). The teachings of Jesus in Matthew 19:12 suggest that He believed singleness is a good thing. As we study the Scriptures we find a number of single individuals who positively impacted our Father's kingdom, including the Apostle Paul, Lazarus, Mary, Martha and the Lord Jesus Himself. If singleness was an acceptable state for the Son of God, how can we reject it?

VIEWING SINGLENESS FROM ETERNITY'S PERSPECTIVE

THE SINGLE SAINT IS TO …

Principle	Accomplished by
Focus their time and energy on their character development (Col. 3:10).	☺ Learning from the wisdom of others (Prov. 1:7).
Acknowledge the strategic position of the home (Gen. 2:21-24).	☺ Studying the culture of the twenty-first century in light of the Scriptures (2 Tim. 3:1-17). ☺ Seeking to be a faithful steward of every relationship (1 Cor. 4:1-2).
Develop a heart of contentment (John 14:1-3).	☺ Maintaining a diligent heart (Prov. 4:23). ☺ Choosing forgiveness and flexibility (1 Pet. 5:5-6).
Manage their home prudently (Prov. 24:3).	☺ Faithfully maintaining their current living environment (Prov. 31:27). ☺ Implementing effective methods of household management (Col. 3:23).
Choose to grow in graciousness (2 Pet. 3:18).	☺ Abiding by standard etiquette protocol (Prov. 11:22). ☺ Displaying gratitude (1 Thess. 5:18).
Practice biblical stewardship (Matt. 25:21).	☺ Understanding and applying basic budgeting principles (Prov. 27:23-24). ☺ Choosing to learn and implement time-management strategies (Ps. 90:12).

VIEWING SINGLENESS FROM ETERNITY'S PERSPECTIVE	
THE SINGLE SAINT IS TO ...	
Principle	Accomplished by
Implement hospitality (Rom. 12:13).	☺ Developing a scriptural attitude towards hospitality (Heb. 13:2). ☺ Focusing on being the host or hostess rather than the guest (1 Pet. 4:9).
Develop a world view (Matt. 5:13-16).	☺ Purposing to broaden their world (Luke 2:52). ☺ Casting their vision beyond their own needs to the needs of others (John 4:34-38).
Accept their unique position in the body of Christ (Rom. 12:4-13).	☺ Thriving in their single state (1 Cor. 7:7-9, 25-40). ☺ Meditating on the fact that God loves them (Phil. 4:8-9).
Practice the Titus Two Principle (Titus 2:1-15).	☺ Willingly practicing the Titus 2:3-5 instruction (1 Sam. 15:22). ☺ Being as excited about being a mentor as having one (Luke 6:38).

22. What Are My Spiritual and Physical Nutritional Requirements?

As you continue to gain confidence that God is your strength, your awareness of your potential to deepen your relationship with your heavenly Father and to increase your ability to fulfill the special plan He has just for you is enhanced! You are more likely to fulfill that plan if you are spiritually and physically fit. How are you approaching the response to this question? Do you have a solid understanding of the nutritional requirements necessary for spiritual and physical vitality or are you randomly starting it without a deliberate dietary plan?

Physically you know that your body has specific nutritional requirements in order to function properly. When you stand on the scale and observe the weight that it records your response may be, 'It is time for me to consider a *diet*—a new plan for my nutritional intake'!

A variety of foods are necessary to nourish you—meats, eggs, grain foods (breads, cereals, pastas), fruits, vegetables, dairy products as well as fats, oils and sugars in moderate amounts. No one food is more or less important than others; they are all needed and they all help one another nourish you.

Read Genesis 1. Each act of creation concludes with the statement, 'And God saw that *it was* good'.

Meats and eggs supply the protein necessary to build strong bodies and maintain body tissue. They are also a rich source of iron needed for rich red blood and the prevention of anemia, as well as the essential B vitamins. The word *protein* comes from the Greek for 'first' and should be the first criteria when planning meals. The grain foods supply vigor and energy because of the carbohydrates, sugars and starches they contain as well as significant amounts of the B vitamins, thiamine, niacin and riboflavin.

Our gracious heavenly Father packaged some of our best cosmetics in the fruits and vegetables He created. Rather than beauty coming from jars, tubes and fancy bottles, a healthy glow from within, the source of true beauty, is the result of a diet that abounds in the beauty foods—fruits and vegetables. A healthy body silhouette is a combination of balancing proteins, fats and carbohydrates with plenty of low-calorie fruits and vegetables complemented with exercise.

Dairy products build and maintain bones and teeth. The calcium and phosphorus contained in milk help calm the nerves. Their protein helps maintain body tissue while the fat supplies energy and vitamin A for sound growth and general health. Vitamin D-fortified-milk supplements the 'sunshine vitamin' which the body produces when exposed to the sun. Vitamin D helps the body absorb calcium and phosphorus, two minerals essential to developing and maintaining healthy bones. A lack of Vitamin D can lead to soft bones in children (Rickets) and adults (Osteomalacia).

Fats, oils and sugars are the 'plus' foods—while they are to be used in moderation each does contribute some nutritive value to our diets. Fats and oils provide the body with energy, bring some of the important fat-soluble vitamins into our system, aid in digestion of essential foods and endow our meals with full-bodied flavor. Sugar provides quick energy and helps the body utilize other nutrients, although its most obvious contribution is its taste, which makes many foods more appetizing.

An intentional spiritual dietary plan is as essential to your spiritual growth as a deliberate dietary plan is fundamental to your physical well-being. 1 Peter 2:2-3 teaches that spiritual growth is marked by a craving and a delight in God's Word with the intensity with which a baby craves milk. A Christian develops a desire for the truth of God's Word by:

* remembering one's life's source ('the word of the Lord endures forever'—1 Pet. 1:25).

* eliminating sin from one's life ('laying aside all malice and all guile and hypocrisy, and envy and all slander'—1 Pet. 2:1).

* admitting one's need for God's truth ('as newborn babes'—1 Pet. 2:2).

* pursuing spiritual growth ('that you may grow thereby' — 1 Pet. 2:2).

* surveying one's blessings ('Lord is gracious'—1 Pet. 2:3).[5]

When you make sound nutritional choices you have the opportunity to dramatically reduce your risk for many health challenges. The same is true in your spiritual life— when you decide to ingest a regular diet of God's Word, spiritual vitality results. According to Psalm 119, an excellent Spiritual Nutrition Guide, God's Word is your ...

* source of blessing (1-8).

* challenge to holiness (9-16).

* teacher (17-24).

* source of strength and renewal (25-32).

* direction for life priorities (33-40).

* reminder of God's unfailing love (41-48).

* comfort in suffering (49-56).

* portion (57-64).

---

5. John MacArthur, *The MacArthur Study Bible* (Nashville: Word: 1997), note at 1 Peter 2:2, desire the pure milk of the word.

* standard for correction (65-72).

* source of consolation (73-80).

* hope for revival (81-88).

* unwavering standard (89-96).

* foundation for wisdom, understanding and insight (97-104).

* direction for life (105-112).

* shield (113-120).

* surety (121-128).

* starting point for understanding (129-136).

* reference for pure counsel (137-144).

* response when you cry for help (145-152).

* deliverance (153-160).

* basis for peace (161-168).

* reason for praise (169-176).

Align Your Thoughts:

The Godly Woman in Progress understands her physical and spiritual nutritional requirements and filters her daily decisions through the changeless instructions found in God's Word (Ps. 119:9-16).

23. Am I Joyfully Using My Spiritual Gifts?

What would be your response if you carefully selected a gift and presented it to someone dear only to have him or her leave it wrapped? A myriad of emotions undoubtedly flood your mind as you consider such an ungrateful response on the part of the recipient. Putting the question in the context of Spiritual Gifts, is there a possibility that you might be neglecting to unwrap the ones our Lord graciously custom-selected for you? Let's identify some principles that will help in identifying and using your Spiritual Gifts to glorify their Giver, your heavenly Father:

Principle One—*gift* is derived from the Greek word *charisma* which emphasizes the freeness of the gift. Your Spiritual Gifts cannot be earned, pursued or worked for; all gifts are graciously given by your heavenly Father (1 Cor. 12:7).

Principle Two—a right understanding of your Spiritual Gifts should evoke a spirit of humility within you (Rom. 12:3).

Principle Three—there is a diversity of unique giftedness. These are distributed to individuals in order to enhance the effectiveness of the entire Body of believers. God purposely planned these diverse capabilities; He never intended for us to all be the same. In fact, to force uniformity is to run the risk of deformity (Rom. 12:4-5).

Principle Four—your Spiritual Gifts were graciously given to you; you do not own them but are simply God's steward of them (Rom. 12:6; 1 Cor. 12:4, 7, 11, 18).

Principle Five— you are to align the use of your gifts with your season of life, keeping your biblical priorities in the correct order (Eccles. 3:1-22).

Principle Six—your Spiritual Gifts are to be used for the good of the entire Body of Christ (1 Cor. 12:7).

Principle Seven—Spiritual Gifts were given to you for the spiritual edification, nurturing and development of the Body. They are to equip others so that they are challenged to move from sin to obedience (Eph. 4:7-16).

Principle Eight—Spiritual Gifts are to be used for the benefit of those in the Body, not simply for your exhalation (1 Pet. 4:7-11).

Principle Nine—your heavenly Father will require an accounting of how you used your gifts to further His Kingdom (Matt. 25:14-30).

Principle Ten—there in no excuse for ignorance in the realm of Spiritual Gifts; you are to be correctly informed about them (1 Cor. 12:1).

Since the Scriptures challenge us to be correctly informed about the Spiritual Gifts, let's briefly define several of them:

* **Prophecy** ministers to others by edifying (building up), exhorting (encouraging) and comforting others in the body of Christ (Rom. 12:6; 1 Cor. 14:1-3; Eph. 4:11).

* **Teaching** communicates the Word of God so that others can clearly understand its meaning (Rom. 2:17-24; 12:7; Col. 1:28; 1 Tim. 1:3-7; 4:15-16; 2 Tim. 2:24-26; James 3:1).

* **Discernment** discriminates between truth and error. It enables us to practice truth that is motivated by love. Discernment provides a foundation for correction in righteousness (Acts 13:6-12; 1 Cor. 12:10; 2 Tim. 3:16).

✳ **Wisdom** provides practical insight into the ways and will of God (1 Sam. 25; Acts 15; 1 Cor. 12:8-10, 28).

✳ **Knowledge** is the ability to acquire and communicate biblical knowledge for the benefit of the church Body (Acts 5; 8:26-38; 1 Cor. 12:8; John 4).

✳ **Leadership** motivates, directs and delegates responsibilities to others. We are to model what we expect others to do in order to stimulate them to love and good works (2 Kings 12:6-8; Neh. 2:17-18; Rom. 12:8; 1 Thess. 5:12-13; Heb. 13:7).

✳ **Administration** understands and facilitates the activities and procedures of others; different from the gift of leadership, the individual with the gift of administration understands how an organization operates, casts a vision of how to increase its effectiveness and guides from behind the scenes (2 Kings 12:7-12; 1 Cor. 12:28; 1 Tim. 3:1-5, 12).

✳ **Exhortation** affirms, builds up and encourages others (Acts 9:26-27; 11:22-23; 13:15; Rom. 12:8; 1 Cor. 4:16; 1 Thess. 4:1; 1 Tim. 4:13; 2 Tim. 4:2; 1 Pet. 5:1).

✳ **Help or Service** lifts others' burdens by extending a 'helping hand' and creates the environment that allows others to succeed in their areas of giftedness (Acts 6:1-6; Acts 9:36-39; Rom. 12:7; Phil. 2:25-30; 1 Pet. 4:11).

✳ **Giving** uses financial and material resources to further God's work and contributes generously, with a cheerful spirit and without second thoughts or regrets (Rom. 12:8; 2 Cor. 9:7-14).

✳ **Mercy** bestows empathy and seeks to ease the hurting and meet the needs of others (Matt. 23:23; Rom. 12:8; Titus 3:5; James 3:17).

✳ **Faith** is the ability to trust God to do what He says He will do. Such faith is the result of much prayer, is accompanied by the assurance that God is working on one's behalf and believes God can and will do what others deem as impossible (Acts 6:5-8; 11:24; Rom. 12:3-6; 1 Cor. 12:9; Heb. 11:1).

What is the benefit of prayerfully using your Spiritual Gifts to their maximum potential? Most often, when you excel the whole Body benefits, and you experience incredible fulfillment—if you are exercising them in a spirit of humility (Rom. 12:3). However, if you compare, force or entertain expectations that are beyond your God-given capabilities, mediocrity, frustration, phoniness or total defeat is generally predictable. So relax and enjoy using your Spiritual Gifts! Ask your heavenly Father to help you cultivate your own capabilities and develop your own style. As well, purpose to appreciate the members of your spiritual family for who they are, even though their outlook or approach may be very different from yours. Simply stop comparing and enjoy being you; to begin the process consider spending some time pondering the following Heart Search!

UNWRAPPING MY SPIRITUAL GIFT …
A PERSONAL HEART SEARCH

❤ Read the passages of Scriptures that describe the Spiritual Gifts (Rom. 12:3-8; 1 Cor. 12:4-10; Eph. 4:7-16; 1 Pet. 4:7-11).

❤ Confirm that you are a child of God; you won't be given your Spiritual Gifts until the salvation transaction is completed (Rom. 3:10, 23, 5:12, 6:23, 5:8).

- ♥ Pray for openness to the leading of the Holy Spirit in relation to the use of your Gift.

- ♥ Examine your desire in the use of your Spiritual Gifts (Phil. 2:13; Ps. 37:4).

- ♥ Identify the needs of your church (1 Cor. 12:12-27).

- ♥ Evaluate your previous ministry-related experiences.

- ♥ Listen to the counsel of mature believers (Prov. 1:5).

- ♥ Identity one thing or action you are involved in that is forcing you to be something you're not. If possible, remove yourself from that activity and see if you sense relief.

- ♥ What happens when you compare yourself with others? Do you find that you don't match up? Do the results of the comparison give Satan an opportunity to discourage you?

- ♥ Are you trying to be something that simply is not you and never will be? Are you willing to accept that your Spiritual Gifts are different and focus on maximizing them to their utmost?

- ♥ Analyze your friendships and determine if you're pressuring someone to conform to your standards or skills. If so, are you willing to back off, let your friend be the person God made him or her to be and encourage your friend to reach his or her full potential?

- ♥ Tell your heavenly Father that you desire to be a faithful steward of the gifts He gave you (Matt. 25:14-30; 1 Pet. 4:10).

- ♥ Remember that heart-searching is profitable. However, one caution is offered; concentrating too much on yourself can lead to discouragement. Rather, focus on the One who is sufficient for your every need (Phil. 4:19).

24. If I Display Gratitude Won't Others Think I Am Victorian?

Thanksgiving ushers in the holiday season. Tantalizing aromas, gala events and clandestine shopping trips consume much of our time from late November to January 1. When caught up in the activities of the holiday season it is easy to neglect one of the most important presents to offer others—the gift of gratitude.

Before the gift of gratitude is unwrapped, may I encourage you to spend some time responding to the 'Gratitude Gauge'? It is designed to help diagnose your attitude toward gratitude. The 'Gratitude Gauge Interpretation' is located at the conclusion of this chapter.

Gratitude Gauge

Place the number that best reflects your response to the statement in the space provided.

Use the following scale:

5 = regularly   2 = seldom
4 = usually   1 = very seldom
3 = sometimes   0 = never

1. .... I quickly acknowledge that expressing gratitude is a biblical instruction.

2. .... I recognize that a complaining spirit is symptomatic of the fact that I lack a grateful heart.

3. .... I understand that cultivating a grateful heart is a life-long process.

4. .... I believe that the condition of my spiritual heart determines my spiritual health.

5. .... I am increasing in my knowledge of the Word.

6. .... I thank my heavenly Father for my spiritual blessings.

7. .... I thank my heavenly Father for my material blessings.

8. .... I thank my heavenly Father for my joyful experiences.

9. .... I thank my heavenly Father for my difficult experiences.

10. .... I offer thanks to others when they extend kindness to me.

11. .... I seek to speak encouraging words to others.

12. .... I quickly acknowledge that sincere gratitude enriches my life.

13. .... I am seeking to serve others.

14. .... I maintain contact with missionaries and seek to share some of their burdens.

15. .... I understand that giving thanks is generated from my will.

16. .... I am aware that being thankful is generated from my emotions.

17. .... I 'pause for praise' throughout the day.

18. .... Others affirm my grateful spirit.

19. .... I acknowledge that how I respond to the biblical instruction about expressing gratitude affects my spiritual health.

20. .... I am like the one leper described in Luke 17:15-16 who returned to thank the Lord for healing him.

.... **Gratitude Gauge Total**

Unwrapping the Gift of Gratitude

The English word *gratitude* is derived from the same word that gives us *grace*. Do you know that gratitude and grace are Siamese twins? Since Christians daily experience the grace of God, and if they look for ways to acknowledge that it is at work in their lives and the lives of others, then they have many reasons to express gratitude. However, many complain more frequently than they express gratitude—and they don't realize what devastating effects their complaining has on their spiritual lives. Though they may temporarily feel better emotionally for transferring their negative thoughts to others, the spiritual toll that the emotional release renders is often devastating.

The impact of a negative, complaining spirit is significant, as the following example illustrates. At The Master's College part of my advising responsibilities included the completion of a 'Senior Contract' for each of my advisees anticipating graduation. Since the task was time-consuming, I eagerly agreed to be a part of the piloting of an online version of the 'Senior Contract'. It was an incredible experience! I quickly e-mailed the programmer and expressed my gratitude for his work on the project. His response brought tears to my eyes—'Thanks for your kind words. I usually only hear from people if they have a complaint!' I was again reminded that the best antidote for a complaining spirit is an attitude of gratitude, and that is something that must be cultivated daily.

The Gratitude Cycle

Did you know that true gratitude expands your ministry opportunities? Consider the 'Gratitude Cycle':

✶ The more thankful we are, the more we are aware of our many blessings.

✶ If we only offer praise and thanksgiving when things go our way, we develop tunnel vision.

✶ If we are grateful for *all* that our heavenly Father brings into our life, then our horizons expand.

✶ When our horizons expand, our ability to sincerely offer praise, regardless of the circumstances, increases!

I can speak with conviction about the validity of the 'Gratitude Cycle'. Many circumstances in my life (abandonment as an infant, orphaned by adoptive parents in my early twenties, being single, to name a few) initially appear as insurmountable obstacles. However, as I choose to believe that my Lord is a sun and shield, that He gives grace and glory and that there is *no good thing* that He will withhold from me **if** I am walking uprightly (Ps. 84:11), I realize that all I need to do is take care of the walking uprightly part (that includes being grateful for *all* things), and He does the rest! Looking in retrospect at the seemingly devastating circumstances, I can now see how my loving heavenly Father used each to shape my character and to enhance my ministry to others.

An Attitude of Gratitude Makes Our Lives a Beatitude

True praise is an enriching experience. It was so with David. As you read his Psalms of praise, you find him thanking God for things in heaven and things on earth. For material blessings and spiritual blessings. For joyful experiences as well as difficult experiences. The challenges David experienced enriched his life because he knew how to praise the Lord. Consider his words …

✳ 'Thou hast enlarged my steps under me' (Ps. 18:36 KJV).

✳ 'Thou hast enlarged my steps under me, that my feet did not slip' (Ps. 18:36).

When difficulties befall us, they only become a liability when we complain. However, if we choose to praise God, those same difficulties will allow our lives to become a Beatitude (a statement of happiness).

An increase in the frequency of praise and thanksgiving is evidence that an attitude of gratitude functions in our lives. When we choose to expand our praise life, expressing gratitude to both our heavenly Father and those who enrich our earthly existence is a reflex response. As we experience this response we can then say like David, 'He also brought me out into a broad place; He delivered me because he delighted in me' (Ps. 18:19).

> ### Thinking Further
>
> ☺ Giving thanks is generated from the Will.
>
> ☺ Being Thankful is generated from the Emotions.
>
> ☺ The Psalms are written to the Will, not the Emotions.
>
> ☺ If I am unwilling to extend gratitude to those I can see, it is highly unlikely that I will thank my heavenly Father whom I cannot see.

Diagnosing and Cultivating an Attitude of Gratitude

So, regardless of the season, are you excited about giving the gift of gratitude? Your results on the Gratitude Gauge you completed as you began to read this chapter will help you respond to the question. Use the **Gratitude Gauge Scale** to interpret it.

Gratitude Gauge Scale

100-90 – a maturing attitude of gratitude

89-80 – a commitment to an attitude of gratitude

79-70 – an understanding of what constitutes an attitude of gratitude

69-60 – a minimal commitment to an attitude of gratitude

59-0 – an attitude adjustment is needed

Align your thoughts

Now that your attitude toward gratitude is diagnosed, consider completing this project designed to help you to focus on cultivating an attitude of gratitude. I believe that as you conclude it you will find that you have many gifts of gratitude to distribute. The impact on your bank account: nothing. The blessings bestowed on others: immeasurable!

* Simple things I am thankful for:

* Specific people I am thankful for:

* Write a note of gratitude to at least five of the names you listed. Place a check mark by their names when the notes have been sent.

* My reaction to Expressing Gratitude:

* Evaluate your **Gratitude Gauge Score.**

* Use the verses that follow to develop principles for increasing your **Gratitude Gauge Score.** An example is provided for you with the first verse.

  ➤ Psalm 18:49—I will choose to give thanks to God and sing praises to His name.

  ➤ Psalm 103:3-5

  ➤ Romans 1:21

  ➤ 1 Thessalonians 5:18

  ➤ 1 Corinthians 15:57

  ➤ 1 Timothy 4:4

* As you contemplate your gift list throughout the year, will you place Gratitude at the top?

25. Is it Possible to Win Over Worry?

A walk through a bookstore, pharmacy or an internet search quickly reveals that worry, anxiety and depression are prevalent maladies in twenty-first century society. Research reports that 2 to 8% of the population suffers from General Anxiety Disorder (GAD). This disorder is one of the major reasons people choose to visit a biblical counselor or psychologist. Women tend to seek help twice as often as men. There is no specific age for the onset of GAD, yet research suggests that it commonly surfaces between the ages of 20 and 40. Symptoms include sweating, accelerated heart rate, dry mouth, stomach upsets, dizziness and lightheadedness.[6]

Panic Disorder (PD) affects 1.7% of the U.S. adult population between the ages of 18 and 54. Women are twice as likely to develop panic disorder. Panic Disorder causes people to feel terror suddenly and sometimes unexpectedly. Accompanying physical signs include dizziness, lightheadedness, rapid pulse, trembling, chest pains, shortness of breath, nausea, numbness and a fear of going crazy or of dying. Panic Disorder can start to become debilitating when the person suffering begins to avoid situations or stimuli in which an attack is assumed to occur.[7]

While the medical terminology associated with worry, anxiety and depression may be new, their incidence is as old as antiquity. Solomon's words, 'there is no new thing under the sun' (Eccles. 1:9), accurately summarizes their longevity. Sarah and Hannah fretted about their barren wombs (Gen. 16;

---

6. Found at www.anxietysecrets.com/anxpanic.htm.
7. Ibid.

1 Sam. 1); Naomi's anxiety caused her to develop a bitter spirit (Ruth 1), while Job's wife's despair was so great that she counseled her husband to 'curse God and die!' (Job 2:9). Biblically the verb *care* (*merimnao*) is used to describe anxiety, worry and depression[8]—behaviors that divide the mind between worthwhile interests and damaging thoughts. The Apostle James succinctly describes the miserable condition of the person with a divided mind—'a double minded man is unstable in all his ways' (James 1:8). Worry generates many negative and no positive results; those who choose to worry allow themselves to become victims rather than victors over circumstances because they chose to 'lean on their own understanding' rather than trusting in the timeless principles contained in the Word of God (Prov. 3:5-6). What is your reflex reaction when circumstances beyond your control occur—do you worry or do you trust?

Just as good physical health is the result of implementing sound health practices, so good spiritual health is the result of applying sound spiritual practices. When we answered the question, '*Do I Know How to Guard Against a Spiritual Heart Attack?*' we established God's Health Plan for a peaceful heart. This plan is the opposite of one debilitated by worry. Recall the four essential elements:

Weight: a need to eliminate unneeded cares (1 Pet. 5: 6-10).

Pulse Rate: the rhythm of one's gratitude (Col. 3:12-17).

Blood pressure: reading of anxiety over trust (Ps. 55:22).

---

8. W.E. Vine, *Vine's Expository Dictionary of Old and New Testament Words* (Grand Rapids, Mich.: Revell), 1981, s.v. 'care, careful, carefully, carefulness'.

Diet: regular intake and submission to the life-giving thoughts of the Lord (Jer. 15:16).

Let's take some time to examine your spiritual health—answer each of the questions that follow using specific examples from your life. They are divided into categories to allow you to assess where your strengths and weaknesses (opportunities for growth) occur.

As I attempt to maintain a healthy spiritual weight do I …

✳ Understand that I have no need to be afraid of my future because God will instruct me and teach me in the way in which I should go; He will counsel me with His eye on me (Ps. 32:8)?

✳ Have the confidence that there is no good thing that God will withhold from me if I walk uprightly (Ps. 84:11)?

✳ Believe God is able to do exceedingly abundantly beyond all I ask or think because the Holy Spirit works within me (Eph. 3:20)?

✳ Trust that God will supply *all* my needs according to His riches and glory (Phil. 4:19)?

✳ Ask in faith without doubting, realizing that the one who doubts is unstable (James 1:6-8)?

As I attempt to maintain a healthy spiritual pulse rate do I …

✳ Have the confidence that the Lord will take care of my concerns and thank Him for doing so (Ps. 138:8)?

✳ Believe that God cares for me because I am His child and thank Him that I have no need to be anxious for tomorrow, since it will be taken care of by Him (Matt. 6:25-34)?

✳ Thank my heavenly Father that He gives me peace that the world cannot give (John 14:27)?

✳ Refuse to waver in unbelief but grow strong in faith, giving God the glory? Am I fully assured that what He has promised He is able to do (Rom. 4:20-21)?

✳ Have confidence that if I ask for anything in God's will, He will hear me? But will I also have a gracious limitation because His will is always best for me (1 John 5:14-15)?

As I attempt to maintain a healthy spiritual blood pressure do I ...

✳ Trust in the Lord with my whole heart, and refuse to lean on my own understanding (Prov. 3:5-6)?

✳ Believe that I will accomplish much if I have faith and do not doubt (Matt. 21:21)?

✳ Focus on the reality that I have no reason to be anxious about what I shall eat, the clothes I need, or where I will live because God will provide all these things for me? If God can take care of the birds and the lilies of the field, then why should I worry about my needs? Am I not more valuable than they (Luke 12:22-34)?

✳ Understand that it is impossible for me to be spiritually healthy and please God if I lack faith (Heb. 11:6)?

✳ Let Him have all my worries and cares, for He is always thinking about me and watching everything that concerns me (1 Pet. 5:7)?

As I attempt to maintain a healthy spiritual diet do I …

✳ Have the confidence that His grace is sufficient for me, for His power is perfected in my weakness (2 Cor. 12:9)?

✳ Consider that it is God who is at work in me, both to will and to work for His good pleasure (Phil. 2:13)?

✳ Have the faith that God is able to do exceedingly abundantly beyond all I ask or think because the Holy Spirit works within me (Eph. 3:20)?

✳ Understand that I am not adequate in myself, but my adequacy is from God (2 Cor. 3:5)?

✳ Believe that because I have been crucified in Christ, I no longer live, but Christ lives in me; and the life I now live, I live by faith (Gal. 2:20)?

Align Your Thoughts

If we desire to be spiritually strong, we will refuse to divide our minds with worry since it:

✳ does not accomplish anything (Ps. 37:8).

✳ is needless to worry because God has everything under control (Matt. 6:31-33).

✳ can only be removed by prayer (Phil. 4:6-7).

✳ is a waste of time (Luke 12:25-26).

Just as worry divides the mind, peace unites it. If you are to win over worry, anxiety and depression then you must fix your mind on your heavenly Father, for only He provides perfect peace (Isa. 26:3).

26. How Can I Detonate Discouragement?

What do you mean when you speak of God answering your prayers? Do you really mean that He said 'yes' to your petitions? One of the most challenging lessons for the woman desiring to allow God to be her strength is to learn that 'yes', 'no' and 'wait' are all responses to her requests.

What is your reaction when you earnestly pray that a situation will have a specific outcome, and the response from your heavenly Father is no or wait? Do you believe that there is no good thing that He will withhold from you if you are walking uprightly (Ps. 84:11)? Do you focus on your responsibility of walking uprightly; or are you like Elijah when he fled from Jezebel to the wilderness, sat under a juniper tree and wished to die (1 Kings 19:4)? The woman who chooses the response aligned with Psalm 84:11 acknowledges that God is her strength, while the one who opts for an *Elijah Effect* is courting discouragement.

Discouragement, extracted from the Greek word *athumeo*, means to be disheartened, dispirited and discouraged;[9] it frequently occurs when there is a discrepancy between expectation and fulfillment. Discouragement's roots are frequently planted in the soil of idealistic expectations such as holding perfectionist standards for yourself and others, embracing impractical outcomes and anticipating unrealistic benefits from work, leisure time, education or marriage. The greater the discrepancy between hope and fulfillment, the greater the potential for discouragement—and in many instances the resulting

---

9. *Vine's Expository Dictionary of Old and New Testament Words*, s.v. 'athumeo'.

emotion of discouragement is actually anger. You know from Scripture that anger for a selfish reason is sin (Ps. 4:4; Eph. 4:32).

A study of Scripture reveals that discouragement was a reaction of many of the individuals recorded in its pages. As believers we should learn from both their positive and poor responses (1 Cor. 10:6) and offer encouragement to others (2 Cor. 1:3-7). Consider the following:

* Cain, when God pronounced judgment upon him for the murder of Abel (Gen. 4:13-14).

* Hagar, after she was cast out of the household of Abraham because of Sarah's jealousy (Gen. 21:14-16).

* Moses when he was sent on his mission to the Israelites (Exod. 4:1, 10, 13; 6:12), at the Red Sea (Exod. 14:15) and when the Israelites lusted for flesh (Num. 11:15).

* The Israelites because of the cruel oppression of the Egyptians (Exod. 6:9).

* Elijah following his flight from Jezebel (1 Kings 19:4).

* Hannah as she experienced infertility (1 Sam. 1-2).

* Job following the devastation of his life (Job 3; 17:13-16).

* David through multiple difficulties (Pss. 41 and 51).

* Jeremiah often called 'the weeping prophet' (Lam. 3:1-21).

* Jonah after he had preached to the Ninevites (Jonah 4:3, 8).

* The mariners with Paul (Acts 27:20).

An analysis of Elijah's life (1 Kings 19:1-22; 2 Kings 2:1-10) provides us with biblical guidelines for detonating discouragement.

Elijah emerged from his experience at Mount Carmel a victor—the 450 false prophets of Baal were destroyed, and the calamity of drought and famine brought about by idol worship ended (1 Kings 18:17-46). Regrettably, Jezebel did not share his enthusiasm over the victory—in fact, she was *very* angry (1 Kings 19:1-2)! Instead of surrendering, as Elijah expected, she issued an ultimatum to him: 'So let the gods do to me, and more also, if I do not make your life as the life of one of them by tomorrow about this time'. Elijah's response is similar to that of many Christians—they observe God perform repeated miracles in their lives—then a bit of minor turbulence occurs and the downward spiral of the *Elijah Effect* sets in:

* The cycle of fear of others or specific circumstances begins (1 Kings 19:1-2).

* The logical reaction is to run from the problem (challenge), instead of facing it head-on (1 Kings 19:3).

* Rather than meditating on God's faithfulness, faulty negative thinking begins (1 Kings 19:4).

* The faulty negative thinking is fanned by emotional and physical fatigue which frequently produces discouragement (1 Kings 19:5-9).

* Further faulty negative thinking yields false expectations and unrealistic attitudes regarding the responsibilities God calls one to assume (1 Kings 19:10).

* These false expectations and unrealistic attitudes can lead to the cultivation of self-pity (1 Kings 19:14).

An intervention for the downward spiral of *Elijah Effect* is essential to begin the reversal process—in Elijah's case, as in ours, the intervention cycle to renew his spirit included:

* Resting and relaxing—too many times when the *Elijah Effect* begins women increase their activity rather than reduce it (1 Kings 19:5-9).

* Seeking solitude to focus on communion with God (1 Kings 19:9-13).

* Using the Word of God as a sword to fight the source of discouragement, Satan (Eph. 6:17). Acquiring God's truth and promises during times of refreshment enables us to engage confidently in battle; for example, Psalms 33, 42, 43, and 71 teach us the hope we are to have in God. Lamentations 3:21-23 describes the downcast man who nevertheless relies on the steadfast love of the Lord. The passage of 1 Peter 1:13-21 challenges us to proclaim the faith and hope we can have in God through Jesus Christ while Romans 8:18-39 reminds us that nothing can separate us from God's love.

* Realizing that refreshment comes through resuming activity. It allows us to focus our vision outward. Balancing the quantity of time invested and the intensity of the activity will ensure that the *Elijah Effect* does not recur (1 Kings 19:15-18).

✳ Allowing friends to minister to us (Prov. 17:17). Remember that being a friend to others is just as important as finding a friend. Accept God's provision for relationships, rather than imposing our expectations.

A study of some of the noteworthy soul relationships recorded in the Scriptures:

✳ Jonathan and David (1 Sam. 18:1; 19:1-7; 20:1-42; 23:16)

✳ Ruth and Naomi (Ruth 1-4)

✳ Paul and Timothy (1 Cor. 4:17; 16:10; Phil. 2:19-22)

✳ Elijah and Elisha (1 Kings 19:19-21; 2 Kings 2:1-18).

Align Your Thoughts

Elijah and Elisha possessed an unusual relationship—one in mind and purpose to serve Jehovah God; they built many memories together because Elisha willingly ministered to Elijah, offering encouragement and affirmation. The loyal partnership that developed compensated for Elijah's discouragement—and when God was ready to take Elijah to heaven, Elisha succeeded him in his prophetic office (2 Kings 2:9, 13). Their adventures to Gilgal (2 Kings 2:1), Bethel (2 Kings 2:2), Jericho (2 Kings 2:3-4) and the Jordan River (2 Kings 2:6) are a reminder that memories require time and energy to create and pose the question, 'What blessings would Elijah and Elisha have been deprived of, had either refused to accept God's provision and perhaps mourned for his own expectations?' As you consider Elijah's life, are you a woman who chooses the *Elijah Effect* or chooses to trust God to be her strength when faced with circumstances that could breed discouragement? Remember that godliness with contentment is great gain (1 Tim. 6:6; Ps. 37:16) while despair plus discouragement equals spiritual disaster. It is my prayer you will choose to detonate discouragement and focus on God being your strength!

27. Why Would I Want To Run to the Roar?

Here is a story that someone told me once about the King of the Beasts. Once he was strong and mighty, but strength and vitality doesn't last forever, so over time he lost his teeth, his claws fell out and he got arthritis in his joints. He could no longer fight to keep his position as leader of the Pride, so a younger lion became the new king.

However, now and then the old king was not entirely useless—he still had a role to play when the lions went on a hunt. Yes, he was old, but he was also mean-looking and quite ferocious. He would stand on one side while the young hunter lions hid in the bushes on the opposite side. When the prey appeared, the former king looked at it and began to roar; the roar scared the prey so badly that it ran to the opposite side—right into the waiting jaws of the hunter lions that attacked and destroyed it. If the prey had run toward the roar, more than likely it would have been safe, since all the old lion had left was his roar.

Think about this story and ask yourself, 'When I'm afraid do I run to the roar or away from it?'

If you walk into a room and the conversation stops what is your assumption? Do you automatically think that they were talking about *you?* Would your reflex reaction be fear of rejection—the source of which is the fear of man (Prov. 29:25)? Or would you trust in your heavenly Father who loves you unconditionally? He promises to give you peace and contentment in the midst of potentially challenging situations (Jer. 31:3; John 14:27)?

Understanding Contentment and Fear
Drawn from the Greek word *arkeo*, *contentment* primarily signifies sufficiency or satisfaction. Scripture teaches that godliness with contentment is great gain (1 Tim. 6:6; Ps. 37:16), God's promises should lead to contentment (Heb. 13:5) and those who seek contentment from money are never satisfied (Eccles. 5:10). Believers are instructed to exhibit contentment in their callings (1 Cor. 7:20), with their wages (Luke 3:14), with their possessions (Heb. 13:5) and with food and raiment (1 Tim. 6:8). Biblically, contentment is exemplified in the lives of:

* The Shunammite Woman, who did not request anything in return for her care of Elisha (2 Kings 4:13).

* Paul, who gained independence from any need for help (Phil. 4:11, 12).

Fear is defined as 'a distressing emotion aroused by impending danger, evil, pain, etc., whether the threat is real or imagined.'[10] We live in a fear-dominated world—

---

10. *Random House Webster's College Dictionary*, 2nd ed., s.v. 'fear'.

serious illness, weight gain, financial reversal, old age, death, rejection and fear of man are all categories of fear that cause a focus away from God and toward the circumstance. Fear is real and it is not always negative—when you sense danger fear usually stimulates you to fight or flee. However, the fear of man is a negative reaction because you are actually reversing 'the royal law' described in Matthew 22:36-40 and placing more focus on loving people (Lev. 19:18) than on loving God (Deut. 6:5). Humanly speaking, this reversal is a natural response because we meet many of our yearnings through loving and being loved by others—affirmation, encouragement, companionship and provision of physical needs. But the potential ability of others to expose, humiliate, shame, reject, ridicule, revile, attack, oppress or harm us physically, mentally or spiritually provokes the fear of man response. As an introverted college/seminary professor each semester I have the choice of allowing the fear of man to affect my classroom performance. Though I have many years of successful teaching experience the most challenging part of starting a new semester is the potential that this group of students will reject me. I have two choices: I can either focus on my heavenly Father's previous faithfulness or I can allow negative thoughts to plunge me into despair. Such a response would undoubtedly lead to failure. By choosing to 'take every thought captive to the obedience of Christ' I continue to excel in the classroom (2 Cor. 10:5).

Fear's Consequences and Antidotes

The consequences of fear are not usually positive—it can ...

* Hinder your relationship with others.

* Stifle your ability to think rationally.

* Rob you of joy.

* Contribute to indecisiveness.

* Reduce your productiveness.

* Create inner turmoil.

* Injure your relationship with God.

Since the fear produces such detrimental results, it seems reasonable to locate an antidote to it. My choice to embrace peace and contentment is based on the truth found in God's Word. I have learned from the Scriptures that

* The natural reaction to fear is panic—the antidote is to replace potential fear with trust in God (Ps. 56:3-4, 11).

* I am commanded to refrain from fearing the reproach of men (Isa. 51:7).

* Since God comforts me, why should I be afraid (Isa. 51:12-16)?

* I can be content in every circumstance because God has promised to never leave or forsake me (Heb. 13:5-6).

Align Your Thoughts

Remember the story about the Old Lion and his roar? Scripture teaches that your 'adversary, the devil walks about like a roaring lion, seeking whom he may devour. Resist him, steadfast in the faith' (1 Pet. 5:8-9). I have learned that Satan is going to attempt to derail the role my heavenly Father has for me in His Kingdom. Several years ago it became clear that my heavenly Father wanted me to relocate. He cemented this direction for me when my Southern California home sold in January four hours after it was placed on the market. Despite the numerous joys I experience in my new environment Satan still attempts to cause me to question my decision. The house sale was one of God's many confirmations for my relocation and allows me to 'run to the roar' and resist Satan's attempt to cause me to be discontent (2 Cor. 10:3-5; Eph. 6:17).

As you know sound doctrine and obey His Word you find that fear is dispelled because Jesus defeated Satan on the cross, thus stripping him of his power and leaving him with his frightening, but harmless, roar (John 12:23-33; Col. 2:11-15; Heb. 2:14-15). If you are going to refuse to succumb to Satan's impotent roar you must replace fear with God's Word (Ps. 119:11; Eph. 6:10-20). As you do so may I encourage you to use the strategy I began many years ago? Purchase a journal and inscribe it with Psalm 103:1--2. Every day record God's blessing to you. Every week review the blessings and as your journal expands return to the blessings of the previous year. I am confident that peace and contentment will replace fear in your life as it has mine.

The only positive fear recorded in scripture is the fear of God. This fear is a reverence of God's majesty, power and greatness; as you embrace the biblical definition of fear you will most likely find the influence of the fear dissipating as peace and contentment fill your heart and mind.

28. How Can I View My Worth Through the Grid of Scripture?

The glossy, full-colored magazine catches your eye at the grocery store checkout counter; as you thumb through it you are once again confronted with the world's propaganda that your worth is based on external attributes and possessions such as affluence, a lucrative profession, the perfect body shape, gorgeous hair, a spacious home, a luxurious car and designer clothes. According to the media external attributes and possessions will provide happiness, and when you are happy you feel that you are a woman of worth.

When asked what their deepest longing is, most women will quickly respond, 'happiness'. The culture of the twenty-first century relentlessly seeks happiness only to find it an elusive goal. David G. Myers, a social psychologist, describes this quest as he writes:

'When we pit happiness against many things that we long for—robust health, social respect, large incomes—most of us choose happiness. Indeed, our search for happiness and for relief from misery motivates a host of behaviors, from success-seeking to sex to suicide.'[11]

What is your response to these questions?

Do I ...

* believe that I am fearfully and wonderfully made (Ps. 139:14-16)?

* strive with my Maker about my appearance, material possessions or professional position (Isa. 45:9-11)?

---

11. David G. Myers, *The Pursuit of Happiness: Who Is Happy—and Why?* (New York: William Morrow and Company, 1992), 19.

* consider that I was created for God's glory (Isa. 43:7)?

* live a lifestyle that declares God's praise (Isa. 43:21)?

* question God about His purpose for the circumstances of my life (Isa. 64:6-8; Jer.18:3-16; Rom. 9:20-29)?

* rejoice that God selected me to be a part of His family (1 Thess. 1:4)?

* comprehend that I am God's workmanship (Eph. 2:10a)?

* bear in mind that I was created for good works (Eph. 2:10b)?

* visualize that I am growing into a finished product (Phil. 1:6)?

* consider that the struggles I experience as a Christian, if responded to in a godly manner, will produce strength of character in my life (1 Pet. 5:10)?

* contemplate that God has worthwhile tasks for me to accomplish until He comes for me or calls me home (Ps. 92:14)?

The Feminist movement of the 1970s profoundly influenced the definition of happiness for twenty-first century women by telling them that 'justice for their gender, not wedding rings and bassinets'[12] makes them happy, and that women long for the freedom to 'define themselves—instead of having their identity defined for them.'[13] Today countless women maintain their quest for happiness and worth outside of the will of God. It is only as they view their worth through the grid of Scripture that they will find their

---

12. Susan Faludi, *Backlash: The Undeclared War Against American Women* (New York: Crown Publishers, Inc., 1991), xvi.

13. Ibid., xvii.

deepest longings fulfilled. It is then that they comprehend that true strength comes only from God. Consider the following comparison:

THE WORLD PROMOTES	GOD'S WORD PROMISES
Physical beauty yields compliments and praise.	'Charm is deceitful and beauty is passing, but the woman who fears the Lord, she shall be praised.' (Prov. 31:30 NKJV).
Performance yields significance or personal worth.	'Then I hated all my labor in which I had toiled under the sun, because I must leave it to a man who will come after me' (Eccles. 2:18 NKJV).
Accumulation of wealth yields satisfaction.	'The rich man said ... "Soul, you have many goods laid up for many years; take your ease, eat, drink, and be merry." But God said to him, "Fool! This night your soul will be required of you; then whose will those things be which you have provided?" So is he who lays up treasure for himself, and is not rich toward God' (Luke 12:19-21 NKJV).
Power and control yields gratification.	' ... whoever of you desires to become first among you shall be your servant' (Mark 10:43 NKJV).
Professional prowess yields fulfillment.	'There was no end of all the people over whom he was made king; yet those who come afterward will not rejoice in him' (Eccles. 4:16 NKJV).
Doing what you need to do to get ahead yields professional advancement.	'He who walks with integrity walks securely, but he who perverts his ways will become known' (Prov. 10:9 NKJV).

THE WORLD PROMOTES	GOD'S WORD PROMISES
Using people to reach your personal goals yields success.	'Let each of you look out not only for his own interests, but also for the interests of others' (Phil. 2:4 NKJV).
Finding the 'right' marriage partner yields happiness.	'No good thing will He withhold from those who walk uprightly' (Ps. 84:11 NKJV).
Promoting yourself yields personal fulfillment.	'Let another man praise you, and not your own mouth; a stranger, and not your own lips' (Prov. 27:2 NKJV).
Asserting yourself yields fruitful results.	' … all of you be submissive to one another, and be clothed with humility, for "God resists the proud, but gives grace to the humble." Therefore humble yourselves under the mighty hand of God, that He may exalt you in due time' (1 Pet. 5:5-6 NKJV).
Enhancing external attributes and amassing material possessions yield the abundant life.	'The thief does not come except to steal, and to kill and to destroy. I have come that they may have life, and that they may have it more abundantly' (John 10:10 NKJV).

As you meditate on your responses to this comparison, how would you reply to the question, 'If you could change anything about yourself what would you change?'

✳ Would your response echo that of the Apostle Paul who learned to be content in whatever state he was in (Phil. 4:11)?

✳ Would you consider that your unique traits, experiences and personality were given to you by a loving heavenly Father for a specific work that will positively impact His kingdom?

✳ Would you acknowledge that the fulfillment of this ultimate purpose is left within your power since you are the one who must ultimately respond to your Creator?

Take a moment to consider the sum of your individual attributes; what do you think about them? Are you using each to further your heavenly Father's kingdom? Remember that as God's adopted daughter your works are to reflect your Father's work in you (Matt. 5:16) and that your body is simply a vessel used to store your inward character qualities (2 Cor. 4:7). If you choose to cooperate with God on the development of character qualities that please Him, you will find yourself focusing on:

✳ your countenance—it should be pleasant (Prov. 15:13).

✳ the cultivation of a gentle and quiet spirit which is of great value to God (1 Pet. 3:1-6).

✳ developing the qualities inherent in love (1 Cor. 13:4-8).

✳ manifesting the fruit of the Spirit (Gal. 5:22-23).

✳ growing in your faith (2 Pet. 1:5-7).

✳ gratitude—the act of the will that gives thanks to God for all that He has given to you (Eph. 5:20; 1 Thess. 5:18).

✳ behaving like His child (Col. 3:12-17).

Align Your Thoughts

Rather than evaluating your worth against the fluctuating standards of the world, direct your energy toward your character first—then you will truly be a woman of worth!

Jesus gave the two most important commandments related to your worth as a woman to a young lawyer who asked, "'Teacher, which is the great commandment in the Law?' Jesus responded, 'Love the Lord your God with all your heart, with all your soul, and with all your mind.' This is the first and great commandment. And the second is like it: 'You shall love your neighbor as yourself'" (Matt. 22:36-39). As you maintain a dynamic relationship first with your Lord, and then with others, you will find lasting happiness and experience a genuine sense of worth that is based on the unchanging standard of God's Word.

29. Why Is Modesty Such an Issue?

Almost as soon as the Christmas decorations disappear from retail stores, fashion choices shift to cooler colors and lighter weight fabrics. While lightening the color depth and fabric weight for spring and summer garments, at the same time the fashion industry tends to minimize the amount of fabric that they contain. As a Christian who desires to please your heavenly Father and acknowledge that God is your strength, you have the challenge of selecting clothing that brings glory to Him (1 Cor. 6:19-20). So you are faced with a dilemma—must fashion and faith be in conflict? If you wholeheartedly embrace biblical standards of modesty, must you eliminate from your wardrobe anything fashionable? Let's take a look at what Scripture teaches.

Fashion Versus Faith—Must They Be In Conflict?

Modesty is a word that is not heard very often anymore—
and when you do hear it, it is often classified as a practice
applicable to the Victorian era. By definition *modesty* means
'having or showing regard for the decencies of behavior,
speech and dress'.[14]

Spiritually, *modesty* is an issue of the heart. If your thoughts
are focused on the attributes found in Philippians 4:8-9, then it
is likely your external appearance will be modest. Perhaps the
following scriptural principles will guide your clothing choices:

* Romans 12:1-2—Christians are 'in' the world but not 'of'
the world. A mature Christian woman develops the ability
to separate herself from an ungodly society. This includes
clothing choices when they are contrary to biblical principles.

* 1 Timothy 2:9-10—clothing is to be modest, with propriety
(or what is proper) and with moderation (applicable to both
men and women). This can be applied to the style of clothes
as well as the quantity of clothes we have; both should reflect
the principle of *modest*.[15]

* James 1:13 —neither men nor women should dress in such a
provocative way so as to entice the opposite sex into immoral
sexual thoughts or behavior. We are children of our heavenly
Father. Since He tempts no person with evil, neither should
we.

Throughout Scripture there are examples of aesthetically
pleasing clothing for both men and women ...

14. *Random House Webster's College Dictionary*, 2nd ed s.v. 'modesty'.
15. See Pat Ennis and Lisa Tatlock, *Designing a Lifestyle that Pleases God* (Chicago: Moody, 2004), 221-257 for further elaboration.

* The garments for the priests were constructed by skilled artisans (Exod. 31:10; 35:19).

* The children of Israel were instructed to attach blue tassels on their garments to remind them of their need to trust and obey God's commands (Num. 15:37-38).[16]

* The Wise Woman of Proverbs 31 wore garments of fine linen and purple (Prov. 31:22).

* The people of Zion were challenged to 'awake and put on beautiful garments' (Isa. 52:1).

* One of our Lord's garments was woven without seams (John 19:23-24).

* The attire for the Marriage Supper of the Lamb is fine linen (Rev. 19:8).

As you study these Scriptures, I believe that you can say with confidence that for godly men and women fashion and faith are to complement one another rather than be in conflict!

Truth in Labeling

When I grocery-shop, one of the items I first look at is the label to determine that I am purchasing the product that best meets my need. As a consumer, I expect the label to provide accurate information about the nutritional value, serving sizes and perhaps how to prepare the product so I will get the best results from using it. I also know that

---

16. John MacArthur, *The MacArthur Study Bible* (Nashville: Word: 1997), note at Numbers 15:37, 38 tassels.

the United States government requires accurate labeling on products produced in America. I would be upset if I purchased a product whose label informed me that the package contained the item described only to find, upon opening it, that it contained a different product!

Just as I assume that the label on a product is accurate, so God's Word challenges me to dress in such a way that my outward appearance is an accurate label for my character. Mark 10:19 says that failure to do so sends a conflicting message to others. As you contemplate your fashion choices, consider responding to the 'Truth in Packaging Inventory'.

TRUTH IN PACKAGING INVENTORY

* Since your clothing is a label for your character, what does it communicate about you?

* What values determine the clothing that you wear?

* When you select your clothing, what are your first thoughts?

* When you dress for the day, whom are you thinking about pleasing?

* What is your response to the question, 'Must fashion and faith be in conflict with one another?'

* How will the 'Truth in Packaging Inventory' influence your future clothing choices?

The Eye Stops Where the Line Stops
The shape of a garment is created by design lines. The actual shape of the garment has a lot to do with your shape. Lines create the mood of the garment. They are either straight or curved. Straight lines tend to look formal, severe and business-

like. Curved lines suggest delicacy and softness. They can make a person appear rounder, friendlier and less formal.

Lines can be used for both structure and decoration in a garment. Structural lines are created by seams and darts—the construction which holds the garment together and creates the fit. A skirt, for example, can be straight, A-line, very full or very tight. A jacket could have a diagonal line or a zipper down the front. Trim, logos and insignias that are added to a garment provide decorative lines. Pockets, collars and lapels create edge lines. Whether the line is structural, decorative or edged, the design principle is the same—the eye stops where the line stops.

When any man or woman allows the line to stop at a private part of their body they may be allowing others to focus on areas that are not meant for their eyes. If they are seeking to glorify their heavenly Father, they choose to only reveal private body parts to the person they marry.

Modesty is Applicable to All Ages and Both Genders

Teaching modesty begins in the crib. It is unlikely that teens will dress modestly if they are allowed to wear skimpy clothing when they are children. If parents dress their children modestly when they are young and set a good example themselves, modesty will probably not become a major issue when they are older.

Given that according to the Scriptures faith and fashion do not have to be in conflict, let's focus on some clothing selection facts that assist men and women in making modest clothing choices.

* Your face displays your character. Draw attention to it by selecting garments that showcase it.

* Tight clothing outlines the body and often draws attention to parts that are private. Provide adequate wearing ease in your garments.

* Tops that expose the waist, hips, or midriff cause the eye to stop at that part of the body. Make sure you choices model the teaching of James 1:13.

* Low necklines cause the eyes to focus on the chest. Select garments that move the eyes to the face.

* Make sure you can sit and bend comfortably in the garment.

* Underwear should not become outerwear.

* Slogans, logos or insignias placed in a private area of the anatomy causes the eye to stop there. Select garments whose slogans, logos or insignias rest against a neutral part of your body.

* Test your garments for wearability. Do this by positioning yourself in front of a mirror to observe what others see:

  ➤ Bend over to check how revealing your neckline is.

  ➤ Sit down and cross your legs to check the length and diameter of shorts and skirts.

  ➤ Bend over to see how high your skirt or shorts move up.

  ➤ Take a large step to examine skirt slits.

  ➤ Place your hands above your head to see how much of the midriff is exposed.

➤ Check what part of your anatomy any writing, logos or insignias emphasize.

Customs of dress change almost with the seasons, and fashions are as fickle as the wind. Wise is the individual who directs his or her energy on ensuring that their fashion and faith always complement one another.

Meditation Thoughts on Myself

The woman who trusts God as her strength …

✳ acknowledges that the condition of her spiritual heart determines her spiritual health and ultimately controls how she responds to life's circumstances.

✳ maintains her body as a precious vessel on loan to her from her heavenly Father (1 Cor. 6:19-20).

✳ understands that to embrace flexibility she must begin with a steadfast commitment to her Lord and her faith (1 Cor. 15:58) and is, at the same time, flexible with His plan for her life (Jer. 29:11-13).

✳ possesses a peaceful heart because she chooses to forgive (Luke 17:4).

✳ speaks with gentleness (Prov. 15:1) and compassion (Eccles. 10:12-14).

✳ recognizes that saying 'thank you' pleases God and encourages others (Ps. 92:1).

✳ casts all of her anxiety, care, discontent, despair and suffering on her Lord (1 Pet. 5:7-8).

✳ refuses to activate the *Elijah Effect* when faced with challenging circumstances (Rom. 8:18-39).

✳ allows trust in her heavenly Father to be her natural response when faced with fear (Ps. 56:3, 11).

✳ knows her sense of worth is based on the unchanging standard of God's Word rather than the propaganda of the world (Isa. 43:21; 2 Cor. 4:7).

✳ acknowledges that God's brand of modesty is always in style (1 Tim. 2:9).

Building My Spiritual Stamina

Continually think about or contemplate the Scriptures that focus your mind on qualities that promote a healthy relationship with your heavenly Father (cf. PHIL. 4:8)

Let the words of my mouth and the meditation of my heart
Be acceptable in your sight,
O LORD, my rock and my redeemer.
PSALM 19:14

Like a gold ring in a pig's snout
is a beautiful woman without discretion.
PROVERBS 11:22

To make an apt answer is a joy to a man,
and a word in season, how good it is!
PROVERBS 15:23

The fear of man lays a snare,
but whoever trusts in the LORD is safe.
PROVERBS 29:25

You keep him in perfect peace whose mind is stayed on you,
because he trusts in you.
Trust in the LORD forever,
for the LORD GOD is an everlasting rock.
ISAIAH 26:3-4

Woe to him who strives with him who formed him,
a pot among earthen pots!
Does the clay to say to him who forms it,
'What are you making?'
or 'Your work has no handles'?
ISAIAH 45:9

Pay attention to yourselves! If your brother sins, rebuke him,
and if he repents, forgive him, and if he sins against you
seven times in the day, and turns to you seven times, saying,
'I repent', you must forgive him.
LUKE 17:3-4

Give thanks in all circumstances;
for this is the will of God in Christ Jesus for you.
1 THESSALONIANS 5:18

Do not let your adorning be external—the braiding of hair,
the wearing of gold,
or the putting on of clothing—but let your adorning be the
hidden person of the heart
with the imperishable beauty of a gentle and quiet spirit,
which in God's sight is very precious.
1 PETER 3:3-4

Cast all your anxieties on him, because he cares for you.
be sober-minded; be watchful.

Your adversary the devil prowls around like a roaring lion,
seeking some to devour.
Resist him, firm in your faith,
knowing that the same kinds of suffering are being experienced
by your brotherhood throughout the world.
1 PETER 5:7-9

Sustaining My Spiritual Stamina

Further study to encourage renewal of your
mind and spirit (cf. EPH. 4:17-32)

✳ Explore the lives of biblical women who displayed flexibility: Sarah (Gen. 18:1-15, 21:1-13; Heb. 11:11; 1 Pet. 3:6), Ruth (Ruth 1-4), The Jewish Maid (2 Kings 5:1-5, 14-15), Mary (Matt. 1:18-25; Luke 1:26-38, 2:6-14, 17-19, 33-35; John 19:25-27), Elizabeth (Luke 1:5-20, 24-25, 39-45) and Anna (Luke 2:36-38).

✳ Develop your own 'forgiveness formula'; begin with the scriptures provided in chapter 9, conduct your own research and then compile the formula.

Write the formula on a card:

+ .... + ... + ... = FORGIVENESS.

➢ Record each time you use the formula; write the occasion and the results on the back of the card (2 Cor. 10:3-6; Eph. 6:17; Heb. 4:12).

➢ Meditate upon the Scriptures and your comments, focusing on your heavenly Father's faithfulness to forgive you.

* Did you know that there are more than 100 references to the tongue in the book of *Proverbs?* Spend some time locating some of them and then follow the instructions for your 'forgiveness formula' to create meditation cards that will ensure that your words give life rather than death (Prov. 18:21).

* Study the life of Miriam, Moses' sister, (Num. 12:1-15), who serves as a graphic illustration of the impact of a sharp, complaining tongue.

MY HOME

Do I Choose to Create a Nurturing Ambience?

30. Biblically is the Home Really that Strategic?

When you hear the word *strategic*, what mental images emerge in your mind? When I hear or read it, I think of something that is important or essential—or a situation that may require that I develop a plan of action. I am also reminded *strategic* is a military term associated with planning and implementing important maneuvers. The Christian woman seeking to make God her strength knows that she is engaged in a spiritual warfare—and that her home is a primary target for Satan's attack. An understanding of the world that her family encounters daily is critical to the Christian homemaker developing an *Action Plan*—an intentional method for acting or proceeding—to protect her family against the devil's strategies (Eph. 6:10-20).

Current research predicts that the nuclear family as we know it will soon become extinct—and Christian families are not exempt from the predictions! As early as 1982, Charles Swindoll presented a grim picture of the family:

> It comes as a surprise to nobody that the family is under fire these days. When one national periodical did a special report on the American domestic scene, the issue was not entitled 'Strengthening the Family' or 'Examining the Family' or 'Depending on the Family'. It was '*Saving* the Family'. Like the prairie bison and the sperm whale and the crane, the family is fast becoming an endangered species. For sure, it is a different scene from the quiet, heart-warming scenes of yesteryear when mom was always home, dad was the sole bread winner, children lived predictable lives of ease and relaxation, and the lifestyle was laid back and simple.[1]

Regretably, statistics describing family life at the beginning of the twenty-first century continued to present a somber portrait—one that the multi-tasked woman must be aware of to develop and implement an effective Action Plan:

* Since 1950 the percentage of American children living in mother-only families has climbed from 6 percent to 24 percent in 1994.[2]

* Twenty-five percent of children will live in a stepfamily by the age of 18.[3]

---

1. Charles Swindoll, *Strengthening Your Grip: Essentials in an Aimless World* (Dallas: Word, 1982), 253.

2. Nelson, D.W., 'Kids Count Overview', found at wysiwyg://68/ http://www.aecf.org/kidscount/kc1995/overview.htm.

3. Barish, Ellen Blum (2000). 'Stepfamlies; multiple marriages lead to blended families' (2000). Found at http://www.wilmingtonstar.com

* The percentage of children living with one parent has increased from 20% in 1980 to 27% in 1999.[4]

* The average number of hours per day American children spend in front of a screen of some kind is 4.35.[5]

* The likelihood of a first marriage ending in divorce is 43%.[6]

* First marriages last an average of 11 years; remarriages that end in divorce last 7.4 years for men and 7.1 years for women.[7]

* At least 500,000 children are physically abused in the United States each year.[8]

* Nearly two-thirds of men who beat their wives also beat their children.[9]

* According to the National Center for Education Statistics, in 1995 there were approximately 21 million infants, toddlers and preschool children under the age of 6 in the U.S.; more than 12.9 million of those children were in childcare.[10] In 1993, 1,802 mothers who were considered 'below poverty' spent 21% of their income on childcare.[11]

---

4. _____, A Population and Family Characteristics. America's Children' (1999).

5. Found at Internet, Netscape Communicator http://tvturnoff.org//factsandfig4page.htm.

6. Found at http://www.divorceinfo.com/statistic.htm.

7. Found at http://www.divorceinfo.com/statistic/htm.

8. Found at www.britannica.com Encyclopedia Britannica – Child Abuse.

9. A Statistic on Domestic Violence. *Women Against Abuse*. Found at Internet, Netscape Communicator, www.libertynet.org/waasafe/index.html.

10. Found at www.tcpalm.com/stuart/opinions/v20snels.shtml Income.

11. Found at www.census.net/familystatistics/children.

✳ Data recently released by the census bureau show that the median income for married-couple families in 1993 was $43,000 compared to $17,443 for female-headed families.[12]

✳ There have been 38,010,378 abortions since 1973.[13]

✳ The number of births to unmarried women increased from 1.17 to 1.3 million between 1990 and 1999.[14]

✳ In 1992, 26 of every 1,000 women aged 15-44 had an abortion.[15]

✳ There were 2 million single fathers in 1997, 50% more than in 1990.[16]

✳ There are 11.9 million single-parents in the U.S. Thirty-eight percent of the children living in a single-parent household live with a divorced parent; 35%, with a never-married parent; 19%, with a separated parent, and 4%, with a widowed parent.[17]

The Christian homemaker's Action Plan to protect her family against Satan's strategies includes creating a nurturing ambience, controlling her thought life, and practicing biblical hospitality. Are you ready to develop

12. Nelson, D.W., 'Kids Count Overview' (1995). Found at wysiwyg: //68/http://www.aecf.org/kidscount/kc1995/overview.htm.

13. S.K. Henshaw, *Abortions Services in the United States, 1991 & 1992* (Family Planning Perspectives, 1994), 101.

14. Found at www.newportnewstimes.com/2000/nt-news0408/ general/nt-news 01.html.

15. Found at www.bfl.org/stats/htm.

16. Found at www.census.gov/press-release

17. Menfeld, Michele, 'Single-parent Central' (2000). Found at www. singleparents.com.

your Action Plan? If so, the answers to the questions that follow offer you guidance and motivation.

31. How do I Create a Welcoming Ambience?

What does the word *welcome* communicate to you? For me, when someone tells me I am *welcome* an image of my arrival being joyfully anticipated surfaces. Along with the anticipated arrival, I picture a serene environment that conveys my presence is valued enough to create a *welcoming ambience*. A multi-tasked woman understands the strategic importance of a welcoming home ambience and carefully prepares her home so that those entering it perceive that their arrival is anticipated. Verna Birkey presented in her 'Enriched Living Seminars' ten principles that are to characterize a home that possesses a welcoming ambience:

* God designed the home to provide the joy, happiness and satisfaction that every human being longs for and needs.

* The home is the place for each to be supremely happy—whether as a child, a wife or as a husband.

* Apart from your personal relationship to God, there is nothing that should afford you more happiness than your family life.

* For maximum benefit to the individuals, the family life must become more and more what God wants it to be.

* You should look forward to going to your dwelling place. It should be a place of order but not a show place. This is important for our emotional and social well-being.

* It's a place where you can bring your friends—a 'Home Base'.

* It's where you feel safe and at ease from the conflicts and stress of the world 'out there'.

* It's a place where you sense you belong because things and people there belong to you.

* It's the place where individual family members acquire an earthly concept of what heaven will be like.

* It should be a place where harmony reigns; some individuals can't wait to get home...others can't wait to leave.[18]

Align Your Thoughts

A sobering question to ask yourself is how many of these principles describe your home? What will you do, today, to create a *welcoming ambience* for all who enter it? A first step is to make your home a place of refuge.

32. Is It Possible to Make My Home A Refuge?

Do you consider your home a refuge from the cares of the world? *Refuge*, by definition, means a 'shelter or protection from danger, trouble, etc.; anything to which one has recourse for aid, relief or escape.'[19] Scripture is filled with illustrations of refuges provided by God; these offer a model for the woman who seeks to make God her strength:

* Numbers 35:6, 11-15 describes the provision made for a place of refuge for those who had done wrong. Is your home a refuge for less than perfect people?

---

18. Verna Birkey, *God's Pattern for Enriched Living* (Kent: WA, 1989), Enriched Living.

19. *Random House Webster's College Dictionary*, ed., s.v. 'refuge'.

❋ Numbers 35:25-28 teaches that individuals are safe in the place of refuge so long as they stay there. Is your home a refuge from physical, mental or emotional abuse?

❋ Exodus 19:4 and Deuteronomy 32:11 portray God as a mother bird sheltering the young and fragile with her wings (Ps. 17:8, 36:7, 57:1, 61:4, 63:7, 91:1-4). Do you offer emotional and physical protection—or is being with you like trying to hug a porcupine?

❋ 2 Samuel 22:3 describes a refuge as a stronghold—a secure, lofty retreat that the enemy finds inaccessible. Are you putting on the whole armor of God (Eph. 6:10-20) so that Satan finds your home inaccessible?

Align Your Thoughts

Biblically, the Lord is the refuge for His chosen ones; because He protects them, they are secure from all hostile attacks. Likewise, the home that is a place of *refuge* is a dwelling where those who belong there are safe from the hostility of the world. As you focus on God being your strength, make certain that cultivating a *refuge* is at the top of your Action Plan. As you do you will create an environment where guests without partners find refuge.

33. How Do I Handle Guests Without Partners?

I was eighteen when my mother became a widow. As an only child I not only had to deal with my own grief, but I also was faced with the responsibility of helping her to adjust to a new lifestyle. You see, when Dad died, she not only lost her husband of thirty years, but she also lost her circle of friends. Suddenly the married couples (my dad was the first of their group to die) didn't know what to do about Mother, so they did nothing. Her grieving process was actually extended because of the withdrawal of her friends, with many of whom she and Dad had enjoyed fellowship for years.

One of the hardest parts of adjusting to widowhood for Mom was being left out of her friends' social events. I knew she still had a wealth of life experiences that would enhance the gatherings she was accustomed to attending. However, she was excluded from them simply because she no longer had a partner. As she grieved over being rejected I mentally recounted some of the gatherings that had been held at our home. The couples arrived and left together and sometimes sat together during the meal or refreshment time. The remainder of the time the ladies were generally clustered together in one part of the living room, the men in another. Since they were essentially functioning as a single person during those times I had a difficult time understanding why Mom was now being excluded from their social gatherings.

In retrospect, I know there were a number of ways her friends could have shortened her grieving process. May I share several with you? These are things you can do to help your friends and guests who do not have partners.

* Intentionally include widows or widowers on your guest list. In the beginning of their grieving process they may not be the life of the party, but your invitation, extended with a heart of compassion, may jumpstart their recovery process. I know this would have been true for my mom.

* Offer to escort them to the event. Even if driving is not an issue, arriving at an event alone can be. Walking through the

door with a friend is a great ice-breaker for the person who is attempting to re-enter their once-familiar circle of friends without a partner.

* If there is a cost involved and finances are tight, offer to pay for or help pay for the event—and assure them that it is your pleasure.

* Keep pursuing them even if they initially decline your invitation. They may need reassurance that they can make a positive contribution to the event.

* If food preparation is involved suggest that you prepare the 'potluck' dish together. This will not only cut the cost for the widow but the fellowship time generated can also be a great encouragement to her. If the widower does not cook well perhaps you can make your contribution larger or assign him something that he can purchase.

* Initially allow them the privilege of reminiscing if they wish to, and do refrain from telling them that 'all things work together for good for them who love the Lord'. That is a true statement that they mentally know but they may need the time for their emotions to match the biblical truth. Consider whether or not you would like the statement said to you before communicating it to the widow or widower.

* Seek to redirect their melancholy thoughts by including them in the discussion of future events—and then make certain they are invited to them.

* Remember, as believers we are instructed to be sensitive and compassionate to the pain and sorrows of others (Rom. 12:15; Col. 3:12)—and there is a 50/50 chance that one day you will be in the same situation (Gal. 6:7)!

There is a happy ending to the account of my mother's loss of her circle of friends! Ever the gracious southern hostess, once the initial pain subsided she continued to extend hospitality even though she no longer had a partner. In the five years that she lived beyond Dad's death, we frequently extended hospitality and eventually our guest list included widows from the group that had earlier excluded my mother. Though her arthritic condition precluded her engaging in as much of the food preparation as she was accustomed to doing, she continued to help me hone the skills that were second nature to her.

The night before she stepped into the presence of our Lord, she prepared a special meal to welcome my friend Carella to our home. As a widow, my mother chose to be an initiator of guests rather than to isolate herself or marinate in self-pity, and in so doing, she left an immeasurable legacy to me.[20]

34. Is My Home a 'Bit of Heaven on Earth'?

When you think of entering heaven, what do you expect to find? As I read Revelation 21-22, my excitement mounts as I consider the inexpressible beauty of the place where I will spend eternity—its radiance will be like a most rare jewel, like jasper, clear as crystal. The city is pure gold, clear as glass, while the foundations are adorned with every kind of jewel. The gates are pearl and the streets are pure gold, transparent as glass. A river, bright as crystal, and a tree that yields twelve different varieties of fruit form a portion

---

20. See *Practicing Hospitality, the Joy of Serving Others* by Pat Ennis and Lisa Tatlock, © (2007).

of the landscaping. Truly, the most beautiful places on earth will be comparable to a slum in light of heaven's grandeur. I don't know about you, but I can hardly wait to get there!

John 14:2-3 teaches me that my Lord is preparing a place in heaven for me—I have a reservation. Matthew 5:13-16 challenges me to make my life and home 'as a city set on a hill which cannot be hidden'. If you and I are going to apply the teachings of John 14:2-3 and Matthew 5:13-16 to our Action Plan, we will acknowledge that our homes are to be the earthly model of the heavenly pattern. Our prepared homes will provide an environment that fosters:

✳ Individual growth and expansion of one's thinking abilities (Prov. 27:17).

✳ Development of personal abilities (Rom. 12:6).

✳ Assumption of responsibilities (Phil. 2:14).

✳ Appreciation and respect for all family members (1 Pet. 3:8-9).

✳ Recognition for personal accomplishments (Phil. 2:3).

✳ Forgiveness of thoughtless actions (Col. 3:12-13).

✳ Sympathetic support and understanding during times of failure or discouragement (Eph. 4:32).

✳ Correction, admonition and instruction in righteousness (Prov. 23:13).

✳ Listening with concern and understanding (James 3:17).

✳ The modeling of the Titus 2:3-5 principles.

Henri Nouwen offers a description of such a home:

> The home, the intimate place, the place of true belonging, is therefore not a place made by human hands. It is fashioned for us by God, who came to pitch his tent among us, invite us to his place and prepare a room for us in his own house.
>
> Words for 'home' are often used in the Old and New Testaments. The Psalms are filled with a yearning to dwell in the house of God, to take refuge under God's wings, and to find protection in God's holy temple; they praise God's holy place, God's wonderful tent, God's firm refuge. We might even say that 'to dwell in God's house' summarizes all the aspirations expressed in these inspired prayers. It is therefore highly significant that St. John describes Jesus as the Word of God pitching his tent among us (John 1:14). He not only tells us that Jesus invites him and his brother Andrew to stay in his home (John 1:38-39), but he also shows how Jesus gradually reveals that he himself is the new temple (John 2:19) and the new refuge (Matt. 11:28). This is most fully expressed in the farewell address, where Jesus reveals himself as the new home: 'Make your home in me, as I make mine in you' (John 15:4).[21]

Align Your Thoughts

Would you consider your home a bit of 'heaven on earth'? As you perform routine tasks, do you monitor your attitudes and activities so that your home is an earthly model of the heavenly pattern? Consider evaluating your Action Plan

---

21. Henri J.M. Nouwen, *Lifesigns. Intimacy, Fecundity, And Ecstasy In Christian Perspective* (New York, NY: Doubleday), 36-37.

in light of your home being a prepared place for everyone who belongs there.

35. What If Adrenalin Is My Stimulant?

Do you ever feel like the faster you go, the behinder you get? Though difficult to believe, the challenge is not the amount of time you have, but rather whether or not you have assembled your God-given assets (Matt. 25:1-30), committed them to Him (Rom. 12:1-2), and trusted Him to multiply them (Phil. 4:13). As you begin to think about assembling your assets, it is necessary to consider the most valuable one you possess: your *time.*

Timely Facts

Take into account the following basic facts about time:

* Everyone has the same amount of time (Gen. 1:3-5).

* God gave His children all the time they need (Phil. 4:19).

* If you are pressured by time it means either you are doing the wrong things or you are doing the right things the wrong way (Prov. 3:5-6).

First Things First

If you are going to use time wisely you must establish priorities and goals. The word *priority* implies that some things come before or prior to some others—not instead of. Priorities enable us to walk purposefully through life with guidelines for making decisions. God's plan of creation provides a priority model—He made animals and man when there was an environment to put them in (Gen. 1:6-27). Priorities provide incentive (Prov. 29:18) and allow us to use time wisely so we are potentially able to make a greater impact for the kingdom of God (Matt. 6:33-34). A Christian's priorities should reflect an eternal perspective and follow the model of the Lord who glorified His Father while He was on earth by finishing the work His Father gave Him to do (John 17:4). David Livingstone eloquently describes this concept:

> I will place no value on anything I may possess except in relation to the Kingdom of Christ. If anything I have will advance the interests of that Kingdom, it shall be given away or kept, only as by giving or keeping it I may promote the glory of Him, to whom I owe all my hopes in time and eternity.[22]

Priorities—More Than A 'To Do List'

Priorities assist us in setting goals—a result that requires action to achieve.[23] Strong people have goals; weak people only have wishes—if your life is going to significantly impact the Kingdom of God you will prayerfully establish goals. Proverbs 16:9 teaches that you should make plans, counting on God to direct you while Proverbs 23:23 encourages you to get the facts and hold on tightly to all the good sense you can get. Elizabeth Goldsmith, a home management educator, writes, 'In the greater scheme of life, goals are arranged in a hierarchy from fairly ordinary to extraordinary.'[24] Writing down your goals and the steps

---

22. *Studies in Christian Living*, Book 6, 'Growing in Service' (Colorado Springs: NavPress, 1969).

23. Elizabeth B. Goldsmith, *Resource Management for Individuals and Families* (California: Wadsworth, 2005), 8.

24. Ibid., 7.

required to accomplish them allows you to visualize the tasks before you and put them in order of their priority.

One Size Fits All?

Numerous resources are available on time management that provide ideas. While they may offer helpful counsel, ultimately each woman must learn what works for her. Generally a variety of techniques must be tried and customized for individual needs—it is important to refuse discouragement if someone else's pat answers do not work for you! There are, however, some tactics that can assist you in assembling your assets:

✳ Prayer is the most necessary, yet habitually the most neglected, tactic in the quest to sort priorities. Scripture teaches that God has promised to provide all of your strength and all of your needs (Phil. 4:13, 19), that without Him, you can do nothing (John 15:5), and with God, all things are possible (Luke 1:37)! Taking the time to petition your heavenly Father to help you prioritize your responsibilities will multiply your time while also reducing your stress (1 Pet. 5:7-8). Charles Hummel, in his classic booklet *The Tyranny of the Urgent*, places this tactic in perspective—'we know that Jesus' prayerful waiting for God's instructions freed Him from the tyranny of the urgent. It gave Him a sense of direction, set a steady pace, and enabled Him to do every task God assigned. And on the last night He could say, "I have finished the work which thou gavest me to do."'[25]

---

25. Charles Hummel, *Tyranny Of The Urgent* (Downers Grove: Intervarsity, 1967), 9.

* Dovetailing or Bunching—this strategy requires creativity since you are combining two or more activities and completing them simultaneously. For example, you might wash a load of laundry while doing a cleaning task close to the laundry area.

* Discern between the immediate and the urgent; there are many immediate but few urgent things, as the life of Paul Carlson clearly illustrates:

  Sometime ago, Simba bullets killed a young man, Dr Paul Carlson. In the providence of God his life's work was finished. Most of us will live longer and die more quietly, but when the end comes, what would give us greater joy than being sure that we have finished the work that *God* gave us to do?[26]

* Distinguish between planning and control; a highly organized person can make things happen. When you are organizing you can be tempted to not remain dependent on God—that is why biblically prayer must precede planning (Prov. 16:3).

* Set aside time to plan. The time that you save will far exceed the time that you have spent in planning. Remember, do not allow the urgent to take the place of the important in your life.

Planning Pointers

* The longer the planning period, the less detailed your planning will need to be at the outset.

  ➤ Plan the predictable. Leave ample time for the unpredictable.

  ➤ Work smarter, not harder—do difficult tasks when at your best, small tasks regularly to avoid bigger, more time-consuming jobs later and delegate whenever you can.

---

26. Ibid., 12-15.

➢ Think ahead—do big projects piecemeal to avoid coming up short in the end since few things really have to be done at the last minute. Take time each evening to prepare for the next day.

➢ Don't trust your memory! Record priorities, plans, appointments, etc. on a calendar, then check it before making a commitment.

➢ Conserve and control time by establishing personal deadlines that occur before the actual deadline. Handle correspondence *once*, taming *all* electronic devices (they should be time-savers, not time-killers). And keep an eye on the three thieves of time— procrastination, perfectionism and poor punctuality— they can potentially add hours to your days.

➢ Learn to live with loose ends.

➢ Reward yourself for completed tasks.

➢ Relax and enjoy life (John 10:10)!

Set Yourself Up for Success

Your priorities, goals and time use are tools to allow you to fulfill the purpose that God has called you to—not your best friend's or next-door-neighbor's. Going against your God-given assets depletes your energy and victimizes your time because you expend efforts in the wrong direction. Successful asset management depends on a sensible assessment of how you operate and what you can handle. The two things you should know about yourself in order to effectively embrace the successful management of your assets are your body cycles and your natural pace.

Understanding and functioning within your body cycle allows you to maximize your most productive days and minimize your commitments on those when your stamina easily wanes.

Dr Hans Selye, the father of stress research, held that we all have a natural pace. Some people he likened to racehorses—fast and vigorous; others are like turtles—slow but sure. He warned against violating either bent—'the difference is inborn. If you force a turtle to run like a racehorse, it will die; if a racehorse is forced to run no faster than a turtle, it will suffer ... every person has to find his own best stress level, the highest level of activity that is pleasant for him.'[27] If you know your assets and ask your heavenly Father to assist you in assembling them, you will be freed from using adrenalin as your stimulant so that you can joyfully fulfill His Will through His strength!

36. So What If My Attitude is Negative?

Are you more concerned about the outcome of your Action Plan or the attitude that drives it? The woman who embraces God as her strength desires to 'walk by the spirit' (Gal. 5:16, 25). She acknowledges that her attitude sets the tone for the home ... in the words of Dr John MacArthur, 'if Mama ain't happy, ain't nobody happy!'[28] Proverbs 4:23 teaches, 'Keep your heart with all diligence, for out of it spring the issues of life.' The woman's inner life determines how she acts. Some questions that may help our multi-

27. Found at www.whonamedit.com/doctor.cfm/2538.html

28. MacArthur, John. Guest speaker for 'Philosophic and Professional Issues in Home Economics'. Fall, 2001.

tasked woman cultivate an attitude that responds biblically to circumstances include:

✳ How do I respond to unforeseen circumstances? (Phil. 4:6-7)

✳ Do I trust God or doubt Him? (Prov. 3:5-6)

✳ Do I trust with increasing grace, patience and love? (Prov. 11:16; Gal. 5:22-26)

✳ Do I respond with pride, greed or bitterness? (Prov. 6:16-19, 15:27; Eph. 4:31; Heb. 12:14-17)

✳ Do I give attention to my words? (Prov. 16:24; Eccles. 5:2)

✳ Do I keep listening to the Lord or push my agenda? (1 Kings 19:11-12)

✳ Do I keep God's words before me? (Ps. 119:11)

✳ Do I keep looking forward? (Gen. 19:12-27)

✳ Do I keep His words in the center of my heart? (Ps. 37:30-31)

✳ Do I think about what I am doing? (Prov. 12:15, 14:12)

✳ Do I remove myself from evil? (Ps. 34:11-14)

Consistently asking yourself these questions and purposing to respond affirmatively will assist you in promoting an attitude of contentment in your heart as you implement your Action Plan.

37. How Do I Create a Spiritual Health Spa in My Home?

When I lived in Southern California I enjoyed visiting a lusciously landscaped outdoor health spa. I only visited

153

it in the summer when the plants were at their peak of their beauty and the gentle sunshine created the perfect climatic conditions. I always returned home refreshed and revitalized. Though I recall with joy those few leisurely days they were an exception to my normal lifestyle. Knowing how refreshed I returned from the spa days, I seek to daily revitalize myself in my home by creating a spiritual health spa. It is simple and low budget!

Be Intentional!

The first step in getting to the spa was to schedule the trip. The destination was a bit too far to spontaneously decide one morning to go. Similarly, creating your spiritual health spa requires that you intentionally designate a time and place. It may change from time to time just as my departure from home did. The point is, I always 'got on the road'.

Have Directions

Once the trip was scheduled I needed detailed instructions if I wanted to maximize my day at the spa. One wrong turn and I would spend much more time on the freeway than at the spa.

The Scriptures—your heavenly Father's special instructions to you—are the directions to your spiritual spa. Saturate your mind with His thoughts, examine the lives of women who are recorded on the pages of His Word and personalize each passage you study. If you will purpose in your heart to internalize the content of your study I believe you will experience spiritual refreshment and renewed vitality.

Pack Your Bag

I purchased a special bag to hold all of my spa supplies. This insured that I had all of the necessities to make my trip memorable. Set yourself up for success by collecting the necessary tools to experience a productive spa experience. Though needs vary for each individual, some common items are:

✳ A notebook or journal—you will want to record your thoughts in a place where they can be referred to at a later date.

✳ Your Bible—always return it to where you study to avoid a scavenger hunt when it's time to commune with your heavenly Father.

✳ Other books you may want to study after you read the Word.

✳ A supply of pencils, pens and other tools like a highlighter—it is handy to store them in a zipper pouch.

✳ Index cards for your meditation verses and principles. You may also want a notebook ring to keep your meditation and principle cards together.

✳ Post-it notes for reminders (especially for extraneous thoughts that distract your mind—write them down so that you won't forget them, but don't allow Satan to impair your time with your heavenly Father by diverting your attention).

✳ A basket, box or other container to store your tools. Graciously inform your family that this box is off limits to them so that you always have the supplies you need.

A Suggested Spiritual Spa Regimen

After my first visit to the spa I knew what regimen worked best for me to leave relaxed and refreshed. The same is true for our spiritual spa retreats. Consider implementing this spiritual health plan:

✴ Exercise your flabby prayer muscles by praying expectantly (John 14:13).

✴ Refrain from ingesting unnecessary 'thought calories' by declining anxious thoughts (Phil. 4:6-7).

✴ Choose a diet of 'high potency thought nutrients' which promote thoughts that are pleasing, morally clean and in harmony with God's standards of holiness (Phil. 4:8-9).

✴ Increase your physical stamina by choosing to rejoice in all circumstances (Neh. 8:10b; Phil. 4:4; 1 Thess. 5:16).

✴ Cast off unnecessary weight by placing all your concerns on the Lord (1 Pet. 5:7).

✴ Accept that you are only capable of cultivating spiritual vitality when you seek supernatural assistance (Phil. 4:19).

If you consistently follow this plan you should possess a more finely toned spiritual constitution that allows you to say,

'I possess spiritual vitality because I chose to
be a Victor rather than a victim (Rom. 8:26-39),
    because I
walk in Integrity (Ps. 15),
Trust in the Lord (Prov. 3:5-6),
Abide in Christ (John 15:1-11),
Love my Lord with all my heart (Matt. 22:27-39),

Incline my heart to my heavenly Father's testimonies (Ps. 119:36),

Thank my heavenly Father for the benefits of being His child (Ps. 103),

Yield myself to the Lord (2 Chron. 30:8).'

(Note that the bolded letters spell **VITALITY**)

Consistently visiting your spiritual spa will produce a woman who, regardless of the circumstances, exhibits spiritual vitality (Jer. 17:7-8) and models that she believes that God is her strength.

38. Are Entertaining and Biblical Hospitality the Same?

What mental images emerge when you are presented with the Bible passages that encourage hospitality? Do you immediately think of the glossy photos in women's magazines—an immaculate home, a gourmet menu or an exquisite table setting? While some of these images *could* be applied to biblical hospitality, what they actually portray is entertaining. Scripture does not give us instructions about home décor, menu or centre-pieces. Let's take a journey through God's Word as we paint a word portrait of biblical hospitality.

John 14:15 and 21-24 clearly state that the primary evidence that individuals are Christians and that they love their heavenly Father is their choice to obey His commands. Though we live in a world that promotes 'have things your own way', I learned that to please my heavenly Father I need to respond to *all* of His instructions with an obedient spirit. I should not just pick those that appeal to me.

One of the ways I can please God is by obeying what His Word teaches about *hospitality*.

✳ Romans 12:13 says I am to practice hospitality—literally I am to 'pursue the love of strangers' (Heb. 13:2)—not simply offer hospitality to my friends. If I want to demonstrate obedience to my heavenly Father, I will choose to practice hospitality.

✳ 1 Peter 4:9 builds on the instruction to practice hospitality and reminds me that my attitude is of utmost importance—I am to practice hospitality without complaining! This verse challenges me to conduct a heart search to discern what my attitude is and whether I am approaching this opportunity to minister with a 'hearty attitude' (Col. 3:23).

✳ I am reminded in Hebrews 13:2 that my willingness to extend hospitality may have far-reaching implications. As we study the lives of Abraham and Sarah (Gen. 18:1-3), Lot (Gen. 19:1-2), Gideon (Judg. 6:11-24) and Manoah (Judg. 13:6-20), we learn that all entertained strangers who were actually special messengers from God. While my motive should never be to give so that I will receive, Luke 6:38 clearly states that the measuring cup that I use to dispense my gifts and talents will be the same one used to provide my needs. What is the size of your hospitality measuring cup?

✳ 3 John 7-8 challenges me to extend hospitality to those involved in ministry for our Lord. It is exciting to know that as I share my home and resources with our Lord's servants I become an active part of their ministry.

✳ One of the requirements for church leadership, according to 1 Timothy 3:1-2 and Titus 1:7-8, is a willingness to allow others to observe them in their homes—the arena where their character is most graphically revealed. Are you privileged to be in a leadership position in your church? If so, remember that these verses are requirements, not suggestions!

The attitude of the apostle Paul is one that all women who desire to cultivate a heart of biblical hospitality will want to copy. As we study the scriptural passages that challenge us to practice hospitality most of us can reflect on a time when we tried to extend friendship to others and were met with rejection. If you are like me, Satan can use that rejection as a roadblock to prevent me from obeying my heavenly Father on future occasions. Paul teaches us that he moved toward his heavenly Father's will for his life—that of Christlikeness. He refused to dwell on the past or to drink of the cup of self-pity but, rather, kept climbing higher toward his goal of Christlikeness all the days of his life. If we are to cultivate a heart of biblical hospitality we must refuse to rely on past virtuous deeds and achievements or to dwell on sins and failures. We must also lay aside past grudges and rejection experiences. Instead we will follow Paul's example and continue the ascent to the top of the 'hospitality mountain'. That ascent begins with developing proper climbing strategies—here are some to get you started:

✳ *Collect and file* simple, inexpensive recipes for desserts and meals.

✳ *Make a list* of people who would be encouraged by your offer of hospitality—purpose to invite your first guests soon!

✳ *Start simple*—spontaneously inviting someone home after Sunday evening church is a great beginning.

✳ *Pray* that our loving heavenly Father will give you joy in demonstrating hospitality to others.

✳ *Remember* that memories require time and energy to create.

✳ *Purpose* to nurture a love for biblical hospitality that sincerely communicates 'come back soon'.[29]

Align Your Thoughts

Extending biblical hospitality is one of the items that is often eliminated in a woman's Action Plan. Are you willing to begin the ascent to the top of the 'hospitality mountain' by including it?

39. How Do I Keep the Holy In Holidays?

What is your reaction when you think of the holiday season? Did you know that the holiday season is actually a 'holy-season' that should bring us closer to the event or person we are celebrating? Contrary to current practice, Thanksgiving Day is rooted in an occasion focused on thanking God for His provision rather than parades, football games and shopping at odd hours. Our study of American history reminds us that the Pilgrims had experienced an incredibly difficult year, yet they chose to be thankful. Christmas is the birthday of our Savior who was born in the humblest of circumstances and gave the best gift ever—salvation. So, what are some ways that you can make this holiday season one that is 'holy'? Let's begin with an assessment of our Holiday Anticipation.

---

29. See *Designing a Lifestyle that Pleases God*, chapter 7 by Pat Ennis and Lisa Tatlock © Moody Publishers.

'HOLY-SEASON' ASSESSMENT

Record the points that best describe your 'holy-season' attitude. Four (4) indicates a high level of agreement.

When I think of the holiday season I …

1 2 3 4   choose to meditate on spiritual truths.

1 2 3 4   pray about events before saying 'yes' to the invitations.

1 2 3 4   Organise my meals beforehand so that when unhealthy food choices come my way I am better placed to resist temptation.

1 2 3 4   prayerfully establish a realistic budget before starting shopping.

1 2 3 4   designate a portion of my holiday budget to my heavenly Father's work.

1 2 3 4   purpose to stay within the established budget.

1 2 3 4   protect a portion of my holiday budget to take advantage of 'after Christmas sales' to reduce the next year's expenditures.

1 2 3 4   am realistic about my body limitations.

1 2 3 4   am reasonable about what I expect from others during the holiday season.

1 2 3 4   create a time schedule for events I am hosting.

Once the **'HOLY-SEASON' ASSESSMENT** is completed use the following scale for interpretation (no fair-looking before you complete it! ☺)

'HOLY-SEASON' ASSESSMENT
INTERPRETATION

40-36   A good possibility your holiday season will be joyful.

35-32   A good possibility your holiday season will be pleasant.

31-28   A good possibility your holiday season will be challenging.

27-24   A good possibility your holiday season will be stressful.

23-below A good possibility your holiday season will generate unpleasant memories.

If your score was lower than you prefer, consider these strategies for moving your holiday season into the 'joyful' category:

Strategies for Keeping The Holiday Season Holy-Season

∗ **Focus on the 'reasons for the seasons'.** The book of Psalms is an excellent source for holiday meditation. Begin today by dividing the number of days you have remaining until December 31 by the 150 Psalms. Purpose to finish the book by December 31. Remember as you read that the Psalms are directed to the will, not the emotions. As you read, underline or highlight each time you read the phrase, 'I will'. When your emotions attempt to control the season, purpose to allow your will to be your reflex reaction.

∗ **Keep a gratitude list.** Use Psalm 103 as your guide to remembering all of your heavenly Father's goodness to you. Record at least one blessing a day (even if it was a challenging day, you are still breathing). Review the list before retiring each evening.

∗ **Maintain realistic expectations.** Remember that your heavenly Father will give you the strength, financial resources, time and ability to create the holiday season He has planned for you. He has promised to meet all of your needs not all of your wants (Phil. 4:13, 19).

Don't confuse excellence with perfection. Excellence you can achieve through our heavenly Father's strength; God is the only One who achieves perfection. Consider meditating on these references relating to excellence while you work—Deuteronomy 32:1-4; Psalm 8:1; Isaiah 12:1-5; 1 Corinthians 3:13; Romans 12:2. Your holiday does not have to be perfect. Remember that approaching a task fretting that your contribution will be inadequate may set you up for failure. Though the fretting could motivate you to succeed it may be at the cost of being so stressed that you or those who are with you do not enjoy the effort you expended.

✳ **Choose to have a forgiving spirit.** Forgiveness is the foundation of all relationships—especially behind the closed doors of our homes. Though the actions of others will at times disappoint us, from a biblical perspective we are to forgive them unconditionally. It is a sobering thought to realize that relationships fracture if we refuse to forgive. When our sinful reactions collide with another's, anger often results. Anger breeds an unforgiving spirit and damages relationships. To avoid that heartache, Ephesians 4:26 calls us to deal with broken relationships before we lay our heads on the pillow at night. Matthew 5:43 teaches that to forgive is the most God-like action possible. God by nature is a forgiving God. We reflect His character when we choose to forgive (Eph. 4:32; 1 John 1:9).Peter generously offered to forgive seven times. Jesus corrected his faulty reasoning by suggesting that he was to forgive at least 490 times! Matthew 18:21-35 clearly teaches that those forgiven the greater sins are to forgive the lesser sins. We practice the truth of these when we offer the same mercy to others that God daily extends to us. Holding a grudge is an unrighteous act. Eventually it will produce a bitter spirit. How many times are we to forgive others? The same number of times we are forgiven—a number that far exceeds 490!

✳ **Set a realistic budget.** List all of the individuals you want to remember during the holiday season. Consider asking them what would be a meaningful gift. Be circumspect regarding homemade gifts. They are fun but often are not useful or meaningful to the recipient. Invest your energy only for those who will cherish the gift. Consider giving the 'gift of time'. A coupon for a meal or child care may mean more to an aging person or a young Mom than a purchased gift. Eat the meal with your friend and ask them to give you advance notice too!

✳ **Expand your holiday calendar.** We have the tendency to think the only time we can fellowship with others is during the holidays. Our calendars are packed solid and then from January 2 to Valentine's Day our calendars are empty. Consider 'post-holiday' events during those cold, sometimes dreary winter months. Purpose, however, to set the dates during or before the holiday season.

✳ **Set priorities.** Focus on what is important and release the 'nice to do but not critical' tasks or activities. Holiday baking, for example, can be a stress factor. Rather than maxing out the oven during the holidays and then letting it set for two months, distribute a cookie or piece of homemade candy in a decorative food bag with a coupon attached that can be redeemed after the holidays. Listing the types of cookies available along with an opportunity for the recipient to list any dietary constraints reduces the stress. As well, if the individual is not a sweet-eater your time and money are not wasted.

* **Work smarter, not harder.** Setting aside specific days for shopping, food preparation and other activities lessens stress. Make lists and use a calendar to schedule tasks to do and events to attend. Refuse to double-book yourself! Share tasks and consider spending time with friends and family while wrapping packages and preparing food.

* **Maintain regular meal, exercise and sleep patterns.** Taking care of yourself will help you cope with the stressful situations.

* **Anticipate a joyful season by meditating on what is right in your life.** Listen to music that relaxes, revives and keeps you focused on the 'reasons for the seasons'.

40. What if I Have too Much Month at the End of My Money?

The events on Wall Street in the fall of 2008 reminded us that no investment in this world is ever secure. Regardless of the safeguards and the supposed guarantees, the economic climate can change in an instant. Like the falling autumn leaves that characterized the season, financial portfolios dropped significantly in 2008, leaving individuals of all ages asking the question, 'Does a gruesome lifestyle lie ahead?'

Economic uncertainty can evoke a myriad of negative responses—especially for the individuals whose trust is in money rather than God. The believer, however, should have an entirely different response if their dollar theology is sound.

Dollar Theology

The cornerstone of *dollar theology* is that believers are accountable to the Lord for the resources that He entrusts to them. The principle of stewardship is woven throughout the New Testament. As you read the following passages consider how they impact your *dollar theology*.

✳ Matthew 24:45-51 and Luke 12:41-48 describe the Parable of the Faithful Steward and remind us that every person possesses natural abilities, wealth and possessions in trust from God. Eventually He will require an account of how each was used.[30]

✳ Luke 16:1-13 reports the Parable of the Unjust Servant. This passage, especially verse 9, is an illustration to show that even the wicked sons of this world are shrewd enough to provide for themselves against coming evil. Believers ought to be shrewder because they are concerned with eternal matters, not just earthly ones.[31]

✳ Luke 12:13-34 admonishes believers to 'lay-up treasures in heaven'.

Jim Rickard,[32] a man whom I greatly respect, is the Director of the Stewardship Services Foundation. This is a privately funded, non-profit corporation established for the singular purpose of serving the fundamental Christian community. Jim suggests a number of Financial Principles to follow.

✳ You cannot be financially bound and spiritually free (Matt. 6:19-24).

---

30. John MacArthur, *The MacArthur Study Bible* (Nashville: Word, 1997), note at Matthew 24:45-51.

31. Ibid., note at Luke 16:9.

32. Rickard, J.W. (Speaker (1991)). *Family Finance Seminar* (CD Recording). Newhall, CA: The Stewardship Services Foundation (The Master's College, 21726 Placerita Canyon Road, Santa Clarita, CA, 91321).

✳ Give to the Lord's work (1 Cor. 16:2; 2 Cor. 9:6-8).

✳ Learn to save money (Prov. 13:11).

✳ Learn to spend less than you earn (Prov. 21:20).

✳ Do not take out loans to finance pleasure items, especially items that are quickly consumable (Eccles. 5:10).

✳ Control your credit cards (Prov. 22:7).

✳ Have adequate life insurance to protect your loved ones (1Tim. 5:8).

✳ Pay off your life insurance by the time you retire (Prov. 13:16).

✳ Have a retirement plan in progress by age 40 (Prov. 13:16).

✳ If you have a mortgage you should endeavor to own your own home debt-free by the time you retire (Prov. 13:16).

✳ Have a workable budget. The key elements to workability are discipline and control (Prov. 24:3-4).

✳ Understand that Tax Laws apply to you—pay your taxes (Matt. 22:15-22).

✳ Have an estate plan that includes a will and/or living trust.

✳ Remember that there is a difference between debt and obligations.

✳ Have cash in an emergency fund.

'Bring the Full tithe into the Storehouse ...'

Critical to the successful implementation of these principles is the application of Malachi 3:10. This verse is a reminder to 'bring the full tithe into the storehouse ...'

To this day I intentionally pay my tithe check at the beginning of the month. And as long as I am also a careful steward of the remaining resources I never have too much month at the end of the money! While God does indeed promise to meet all of our needs, He also calls us to exercise faithful financial stewardship with our resources. Learning to manage your money is a significant component of faithful financial stewardship.

Managing Your Money

You may be inclined to laugh when managing your financial resources is mentioned since you may think that you do not have many. However, everyone has some resources that they need to manage regardless of their season of life. Several statistics remind us of the need to cultivate sound financial stewardship:

> In the U.S. 57% of divorced couples named money as the cause. Several authorities from the law and finance industries discuss why finances cause so many marital problems. Different financial goals and views of the role of money as well as a simple lack of money are some of the causes of discord.[33]

If you have an annual income of over $50,000, your risk of divorce decreases by 30%.[34]

Failing to have a budget or spending plan is like trying to navigate through an unfamiliar city without a road map. You most likely will get lost. Recall the teaching of

---

33. Found at http://www.highbeam.com/doc/1G1-8930297.html

34. Found at http://www.divorce.lovetoknow.com/Divorce_Statistics

Proverbs 29:18, 'Where there is no prophetic vision the people cast off restraint, (or the people are discouraged).'

A *budget* or *spending plan* is simply a road map for using the money you have to its maximum potential. Designing a personal *budget*, or *spending plan*, is not difficult. However, to build a successful *budget* you must know your personal goals and determine your expenses.

Setting Personal Goals

Every successful spending plan is based on clearly defined personal goals—the things you really want. They can be short-term, like saving for a new pair of shoes, or long-term, such as having enough money to make the down payment on a home. Most goals require more money than what you have right now. That is why goals must be written down. Once they are in place then you are ready to build your budget.

Building Your Budget

Consider using the following steps to build your budget.

✳ Pray! (John 14:13; John 15:16; 1 Pet. 5:7-8; James 1:5)

✳ List your income and expenses to develop your budget or spending plan.

✳ You must know the following information to be successful:

  ➤ *Your income*—salary, retirement benefits, gifts and loans.

  ➤ *Fixed Expenses*—tithing, house payment or rent, car insurance, gas, utilities, etc.

  ➤ *Variable Expenses*—clothing, entertainment, gifts, etc.

➤ *Savings*—an established percentage of each paycheck. Since we learn to get along with what we have, this should be determined before any money is spent from the first paycheck.

✳ Create a Weekly Spending Plan.

➤ Once your income and expenses are determined you need to chart them weekly.

➤ This step allows you to develop a *spending plan* or *budget*.

➤ Once you have charted your expenses for a month you need to evaluate it to determine whether or not it is helping you to reach your personal goals.

➤ Revision is necessary if there is too much week at the end of the money.

As you think of your finances, would you be considered a faithful steward? Regardless of your response, completing the following activities can assist you in **Building A Spiritual Bank Account.**

✳ Conduct a scripture search on the word *money*. Use a concordance (either book or electronic). Create a chart like the one below to record your research.

SCRIPTURE	WHAT THE VERSE SAYS TO ME
1 Corinthians 4:1-2	I am to be a good manager of all of the resources God has given to me.

✳ Review the principles listed in 'The Dollar Theology' sub-heading. What do they teach you about money and how you should use it? Develop a personal 'Dollar Theology'. Some verses to launch your study are Proverbs 11:24, 13:11; Ecclesiastes 5:10; Malachi 3:10; Matthew 6:24; Mark 12:40-42; Luke 6:38; 2 Corinthians 9:6-8; 1 Timothy 6:10.

✳ What is your response to the spiritual investment principle which states 'all that we have belongs to the Lord'?

41. How Can My Home Become a Center for Evangelism?

Do you know the birthplace of *evangelism*? Since the twenty-first century church has cultivated highly sophisticated procedures and tools for *evangelism*—training sessions, videos, seminars, manuals and methodology books—it seems logical that the church was its birthplace. However, a study of church history reveals it was the home, not the church that served as the center for *evangelism* in the early expansion of Christianity. Michael Green writes, 'One of the most important methods of spreading the gospel in antiquity was the use of homes.'[35] He then affirms the home of Aquila and Priscilla by stating, 'Homes like this must have been exceedingly effective in the evangelistic outreach of the church.'[36]

Vonette Bright, who along with her husband, Bill, founded Campus Crusade for Christ in 1951, encourages Christian women to use their homes as a center for evangelism. Writing in *The Joy of Hospitality*, she explains how hospitality can build bridges to those who need Christ ...

> Hospitality is more than entertaining. It is expecting God to do great things through you as you reach out to

---

35. Michael Green, *Evangelism in the Early Church* (Grand Rapids: Eerdmans, 1970), p.236.

36. Ibid., p. 207.

touch the lives of others. It is focusing our relationships, especially the greatest relationship of all—walking and talking with the Lord Jesus Christ. True hospitality doesn't wear us out or make us feel pressured; life-sharing is not entertaining in our own strength. It flows from a heart full of love for others. Christ's love, which doesn't come from our self-effort, is a work of the Holy Spirit in our lives. The love of Christ is what draws people to God. This love transforms a party or other event into true hospitality. Hospitality, then, is not an event, it is genuine concern for another's well-being.[37]

An excursion through New Testament Scriptures gives us insight into the importance of *evangelism* for the believer:

* Our Lord's final instruction to His disciples was to make disciples, not merely converts, of all nations (Matt. 28:19).

* Paul writes that our Lord gave spiritual gifts, including the gift of being an *evangelist*, to those He called into service (Eph. 4:11). Repeating the term in 2 Timothy 4:5, Paul directs believers 'to do the work of an *evangelist*'. John MacArthur provides insight on this passage by defining *evangelist* for us:

Used only two other times in the NT (Acts 21:8; Eph. 4:11), this word always refers to a specific office of ministry for the purpose of preaching the gospel to non-Christians. Based on Ephesians 4:11, it is very basic to assume that all churches would have both pastor-teachers and evangelists. But the related verb 'to preach the gospel' and the related noun 'gospel' are used throughout the NT not only in relation to evangelists, but also to the call for every Christian, especially

---

37. Vonette Bright, *The Joy of Hospitality* (Orlando: Lifeway, 1996), p. 32.

preachers and teachers, to proclaim the gospel. Paul did not call Timothy to the office of an evangelist, but to 'do the work' of one.[38]

Align Your Thoughts

As with the concept of our homes becoming places of *refuge* for others, they become *centers for evangelism* when they are dedicated to our Lord; unlimited opportunities exist—as you multi-task, as a part of your Action Plan. Will you purpose to create a *Center for Evangelism* in your home?

Meditation Thoughts on My Home

The woman who trusts God as her strength …

✳ understands the strategic position of her home (Matt. 5:13-16).

✳ cultivates a home that emanates a welcoming ambience (Prov. 31:27).

✳ as she multi-tasks, makes certain that cultivating the attributes of the *welcoming home* are at the top of her Action Plan (Prov. 14:1).

✳ monitors her tasks so that her home is an earthly model of the heavenly pattern (John 14:2-3).

✳ chooses to see beyond the imperfections of those residing in her home (Phil. 4:8-9).

✳ acknowledges that her attitude sets the tone for the home (Prov. 4:20-27).

---

38. John MacArthur, *The MacArthur Study Bible* (Nashville: Word, 2000), notes at 2 Timothy 4:5.

✳ believes that the spiritually happy woman is characterized by the consistent contemplation and internalization of God's Word (Ps. 1:2).

✳ eagerly embraces the instructions to practice biblical hospitality (Rom. 12:13b, 1 Tim. 3:1-2, Titus 1:7-8, Heb. 13:2, 1 Pet. 4:9).

✳ purposes to create a *Center for Evangelism* in her home (2 Tim. 4:5).

✳ cultivates the heart of a Christian hostess (Heb. 13:2).

Building My Spiritual Stamina

Continually think about or contemplate the Scriptures that focus your mind on qualities that promote godly homes (cf. PHIL. 4:8)

Unless the LORD builds the house, those who build it labor in vain
PSALM 127:1

The wisest of women builds her house, but folly with her own hands tears it down
PROVERBS 14:1

She looks well to the ways of her household and does not eat the bread of idleness
PROVERBS 31:27

In my Father's house are many rooms. If it were not so, would I have told you that I go to prepare a place for you? And if I go and prepare a place for you,

I will come again and will take you to myself,
that where I am you may be also
JOHN 14:2-3

Contribute to the needs of saints and seek to show hospitality
ROMANS 12:13

The saying is trustworthy:
if anyone aspires to the office of overseer, he
desires a noble task.
Therefore an overseer must be above reproach, the
husband of one wife,
sober-minded, self-controlled, respectable, hospitable …
1 TIMOTHY 3:1-2

Do not neglect to show hospitality to strangers,
for thereby some have entertained angels unawares
HEBREWS 13:2

Show hospitality to one another without grumbling
1 PETER 4:9

Sustaining My Spiritual Stamina

Further study to encourage renewal of your
mind and spirit (cf. EPH. 4:17-32)

✳ Write a description of your home. What would be your family's reaction to the statement, 'some individuals can't wait to get home...others can't wait to leave'? Establish an Action Plan that will cultivate a welcoming environment in your home.

✳ Study the book of Psalms and record the references to the Lord being a source of refuge using a chart format. Personalize the reference by setting goals for your own home.

THE LORD IS ... REFERENCE AND CONTENT	PERSONAL APPLICATION TO MY HOME
Psalm 18:2-3 - the Lord is my rock, my fortress, my deliverer, my strength ... in whom I can trust. He is a shield to all those who put their trust in Him.	I will choose to create a trustworthy environment in my home. I will trust in the Lord and not my own understanding to make this a reality.

✳ Using 'How Do I Create a Spiritual Health Spa in My Home?' as a guide, create a Spiritual Health Spa in Your Home.

SUGGESTED RESOURCES

Debt-Proof Living Website – http://www.cheapskatemonthly.com

Ennis, Pat & Tatlock, Lisa. (2003). *Becoming a Woman Who Pleases God: A Guide to Developing Your Biblical Potential* (Chapter Six). Chicago: Moody.

Ennis, Pat & Tatlock, Lisa. (2004). *Designing a Lifestyle that Pleases God, A Practical Guide* (Chapter Six). Chicago: Moody.

Hunt, Mary. (2005). *Debt-Proof Living*. Los Angeles, CA: DPL Press, Inc.

Hunt, Mary. (2005). *Live Your Life for Half the Price*. Los Angeles, CA: DPL Press, Inc.

MacArthur, John. (2000). *Whose Money Is It Anyway?* Nashville, TN: Word Publishing.

Quicken Offices – 2632 Marine Way, Mountain View, CA 94043 (www.quicken.com)

MY WORLD

Am I Cultivating A Personal World View?

42. How Broad is My World?

As a woman seeking to make God your strength, is one of your goals to be both salt and light to a decaying world? If so, you will want to ask yourself the question, 'How broad is my world?' If your response is 'broad', then as opportunities emerge you will rarely find yourself lacking an accurate knowledge of topics under discussion in a group of well-informed people. If you are up to date with current events then you avoid the how-ignorant-and-uninformed-I-am syndrome. As an informed person you stimulate your mind by keeping your heart and eyes open to the multifaceted dimensions of life that arouse your interest, delight your soul and provide an opportunity for ministry. Elizabeth George challenges us in *A Woman After God's Own Heart* to broaden our world by creating 'Five Fat Files'. She introduces her challenge by stating,

> In addition to being our Savior, Jesus is our model for how to live a life that pleases God. When we look at His life, we see that 'Jesus increased in wisdom' (Luke 2:52). One proverb (a constant challenge to me) reflects the importance of such growth: 'The heart of him who has understanding seeks knowledge, but the mouth of fools feeds on foolishness' (Prov. 15:14). Put another way, an intelligent person purposefully seeks knowledge, but fools nibble randomly, vacantly chewing on words and ideas that have no value, no flavor and no nutrition.
>
> What are you and I feeding our mind? Are we heeding this biblical warning about the danger of 'garbage in, garbage out'? May we *purposefully* seek knowledge and guard against spending precious time on things that have no value. One way I guard my mind is by following the advice of a special woman, advice which has provided fodder for teaching, books, study materials and ministry. She told me, 'Liz, you've got to have five fat files!'

She then provides a workable strategy …

> *Create five fat files*– Purchase five manila file folders.

> *Aim at expertise*– Next, select five areas you'd like to become an expert in and label a file for each of them. A word of caution: choose areas from the spiritual realm. Remember the proverb? You don't want to feed on pursuits that have no value. Instead choose topics of eternal value. To help you determine those five areas, answer the questions 'What do you want to be known for?' and 'What topic do you want your name associated with?'

Fill the files– Now start putting information into your files. They'll get fat as you follow the exhortation to 'read everything on [your] subject … articles, books, specialized magazines, and news clippings … attend seminars … teach on the subject(s) … spend time with those who are the best in these areas, picking their brains … seek and sharpen your expertise.'

A woman who desires God to be her strength will develop a personal worldview by cultivating her mind and elevating her thoughts so she is capable of conversing knowledgably on current topics. Grasping the principle of 'salt and light', choosing to embrace impartiality, learning about God through orphans, visualizing her profession as a high calling and walking worthy of it, and choosing to follow the role model of biblical women are areas that will assist in its cultivation. Let's explore how to cultivate each area in the question responses that follow.

43. Is Salt Always a Culprit in Our Diet?

Salt receives much bad press in today's nutritional literature—and rightfully so! Nutrition research reports that 'the minimum sodium requirement for adults is 500 milligrams per day. The average adult consumes 4000 to 7000 milligrams of sodium or more daily—and much of it is provided through processed foods and salt added in cooking and at the table.'[1] Hypertension (high blood pressure) and loss of calcium retention is often the result—a condition prevalent among all ages in the twenty-first century.

1. Wardlaw, Gordon M. *Contemporary Nutrition, Issues and Insights* (New York: McGraw-Hill, 2003), 299-302.

So is salt always a culprit in our diet? Nutritional research reveals that some salt intake is necessary, since it aids nerve impulse transmission and water balance. Biblically, a study of Scripture reminds us that 'salt is one of the most commonly used seasonings in antiquity (Job 6:6). Its preservative powers made it an absolute necessity of life and, not surprisingly, endowed it with religious significance. Salt was used for Israelite worship to season incense (Exod. 30:35) and all offerings were to be seasoned with salt (Lev. 2:13; Ezek. 43:24). Numbers 18:19 and 2 Chronicles 13:5 find salt symbolizing the making of a covenant. Jesus, in the Sermon on the Mount, calls the people who listen to Him "the salt of the earth" (Matt. 5:13).'[2] *The MacArthur Study Bible* offers a useful description of the phrase 'if the salt loses its flavor, how shall it be seasoned?'

> Salt is both a preservative and a flavor enhancer. No doubt its use as a preservative was Jesus' primary concern. Pure salt cannot lose its flavor or effectiveness, but the salt that is common in the Dead Sea area is contaminated with gypsum and other minerals and may have a flat taste or be ineffective as a preservative. Such mineral salts were useful for little more than keeping footpaths free of vegetation.[3]

And, what about light? If you have ever been in an environment that was suddenly plunged into total darkness without a flashlight or candles, you certainly know its importance.

---

2. Achtemier, Paul J. *Harper's Bible Dictionary* (San Francisco: Harper and Row Publishers, Inc.), s.v. 'salt'.

3. MacArthur, John. *The MacArthur Study Bible* (Nashville: Word, 1997), 1400.

Biblically, 'light is the word used in connection with joy, blessing and life in contrast to sorrow, adversity and death. At an early time it came to signify God's presence and favor (Ps. 27:1; Isa. 9:2; 2 Cor. 4:6) in contrast to God's judgment (Amos 5:18).'[4] The principle of 'salt and light' is derived from combining the preserving power of the salt with the joy and blessing derived from light. The presence of the woman drawing strength from her heavenly Father produces joy and blessing and at the same time offers a savoring and preserving influence.

The principle of 'salt and light' radiates from the life of this woman. As she focuses on casting her vision beyond her own needs to the needs of others (John 4:34-38), she is challenged to incorporate the model of the homes of the citizens of the ancient East that left a light burning through the night (Prov. 31:18). The light burning indicated a haven for the distressed and signified prosperity. While perhaps not leaving a literal light on throughout the night, her home is known as a haven for the physically and emotionally distressed. Developing effective management skills allows her to maintain her priorities in such a way that she possesses the physical and spiritual resources to assist others (Jer. 17:1-8). The application of the Titus 2:3-5 principle challenges her to concentrate her ministry efforts first on those residing in her home and then on to those beyond her household—and because of the 'family-first priority' their home serves as a preserving institution of society as well as a lighthouse to point others to the saving power of Christ (John 3:16).

---

4. *The New Bible Dictionary*, s.v. 'light'.

Rebecca Pippert's writings in *Out of the Saltshaker and into the World* reinforce evangelism as a way of life; in the preface to the book she proposes:

> Jesus tells us in the Sermon on the Mount that we are the salt of the earth. And he challenges us not to lose our savor—our saltiness. This means—among other things—that we are to be active in the world as his representatives. We are to get out of the saltshaker and into life itself. Not to be trodden down, but to be zestful witnesses to Jesus as Lord and Savior, as the one who alone gives life and meaning to a dying world.[5]

May I encourage you to mobilize your home to function as a saltshaker spreading its contents to a decaying world desperately needing its preserving contents? Hospitality is one vehicle to begin the 'seasoning process'. The Scriptures record that God used food in special ways to carry out His will and show His grace:

* Esau sold his birthright for a bowl of stew (Gen. 25:29-34; Heb. 12:16).

* Jacob sent his sons to Egypt to buy grain and found Joseph (Gen. 41-46).

* Abraham and Sarah made a meal for strangers and entertained angels unaware (Gen. 18:1-22; Heb. 13:2).

* When the Israelites went to spy out the land, they came back with reports about the food (Num. 13:26-33).

* The birds fed Elijah (1 Kings 17:2-7).

---

5. Pippert, Mary. *Out of the Saltshaker and into the World* (Downers Grove: Inter-varsity Press, 1979), 11-12.

✳ The widow of Zarephath shared her food, which caused a supernatural multiplication (1 Kings 17:8-16).

✳ And the greatest blessing—all Christians will be guests at the Marriage Feast of the Lamb (Rev. 19:7-10)!

So, are you ready to begin the 'salt and light mobilization process'? Will you ask your heavenly Father to allow your home to be a 'prepared place' (John 14:2-3) for your family and a 'city that is set on a hill' (Matt. 5:14-16) for those who observe your life? By doing so you will find yourself well on the way to being a salty, light-generating woman!

44. Am I Willing to Embrace Impartiality?

As a young professional unfamiliar with the dynamics of the inner workings of college life, I was both amazed and delighted when I received a phone call from the Academic Vice President's wife inviting me to ride with her and a group of ladies to a function for women of the college. New to the institution herself, her gentle Southern drawl warmly invited me to 'come and ride with us'; I was immediately impressed by the warmth she projected. Throughout her years as the 'Academic First Lady', Melinda's graciousness and impartiality among our college family, as well as the church that sponsored the institution, provided a unifying force. Even when the dark shadow of divorce fell across the life that she knew as the 'Academic First Lady', her gracious poise and trust in her heavenly Father served as an incredible role model for those who knew her. Because she embraced graciousness and impartiality throughout her tenure, her support group was drawn from a wide assortment of ages, professional standings and social circles.

Graciousness and *impartiality* are Siamese twins. Graciousness is blatantly absent in twenty-first century Christian culture which suggests that the incidence of impartiality is most likely missing as well. *Gracious* is defined as being kindly disposed or showing favor and mercy to someone, usually by a person of superior position and power. Scriptural instances portray Potiphar dealing graciously with Joseph (Gen. 39:4), Ruth finding favor in the eyes of Boaz (Ruth 2:10) and King Ahasuerus' gracious treatment of Esther (Esther 2:17; 5:2). Biblically, our heavenly Father sets the standard for graciousness toward human beings, as stated in the ancient liturgical formula: 'The Lord, the Lord God, merciful and gracious, slow to anger, and abounding in steadfast love and faithfulness' (Exod. 34:6). Psalm 86:15 portrays God as 'full of compassion, and gracious, longsuffering and abundant in mercy and truth' (nkjv). Psalm 103:8 declares, 'The Lord is merciful and gracious, slow to anger, and abounding in mercy' (nkjv) while Psalm 145:8 affirms, 'The Lord is gracious and full of compassion, slow to anger and great in mercy' (nkjv).

Impartiality by definition means not partial or biased;[6] to understand impartiality you must first define partial— which, from a biblical perspective, 'originally referred to raising someone's face or elevating someone strictly on a superficial, external basis, such as appearance, race, wealth, rank or social status.'[7] James 2:1-17 passionately challenges Christians to shun the sin of partiality (2:9) by focusing

6. *Random House Webster's College Dictionary*, 2nd ed., s.v. 'impartial'.

7. John MacArthur, *The MacArthur Study Bible* (Nashville: Word, 1997), note at James 2:1.

on how the Lord Jesus, the King of the Universe, chose to make His advent on earth:

* He was born in a stable (Luke 2:7)

* Possessed a less than impressive genealogy (Matt. 1:1-16)

* Lived in the humble village of Nazareth for thirty years (Matt. 2:19-23; Luke 2:39)

* Selected men engaged in a variety of professions for his disciples (Matt. 4:18-22; Mark 1:16-20)

* Ministered in Galilee and Samaria, two communities notoriously held in contempt by Israel's leaders (John 4)

* Ate with tax collectors and sinners (Matt. 9:10-12)

* Associated with women of questionable reputation (John 4:1-26, 8:1-11).

James compares the church's reaction to the rich and the poor (2:2-4) and concludes that the church is to be a classless society, since its primary concern is to fulfill the royal law and love your neighbor as yourself (2:8).'James is not advocating some kind of emotional affection for oneself—self-love is clearly a sin (2 Tim. 3:2). Rather, the command is to pursue meeting the physical health and spiritual well-being of one's neighbors (all within the sphere of our influence; Luke 10:30-37) with the same intensity and concern as one does naturally for one's self (Phil. 2:3-4).'[8]

As you concentrate on fulfilling the royal law and loving your neighbor as yourself, you will want to consider 'the neighbors' whom you could demonstrate impartiality

---

8. John MacArthur, *The MacArthur Study Bible* (Nashville: Word, 1997), note at James 2:8

to—singles, widows and individuals experiencing food insecurity (low-incomes, poverty level and the homeless).

Single is defined as 'pertaining to the unmarried state'. The October 20, 2003 cover story of *Business Week* reports that

> The U.S. Census Bureau's newest numbers show that married-couple households—the dominant cohort since the country's founding—have slipped from nearly 80% in the 1950s to just 50.7% today. That means that the U.S.'s 86 million single adults could soon define the new majority. Already, unmarrieds make up 42% of the workforce, 40% of homebuyers, 35% of voters, and one of the most potent—if pluralistic—consumer groups on record.[9]

When you plan social gatherings do you embrace impartiality and include singles? More than likely their life experiences are rich, and they will enhance your social gathering. A widow is 'a woman who has lost her husband by death and has not remarried'. Read 1 Timothy 5:3-16. This passage provides a clear definition of a Christian widow and specific instructions on how the church is to respond to her if she has no means of providing for her daily needs. National Bereavement Statistics reported by the American Association of Retired People (AARP) tell us that:

✳ In 1999 almost half (45%) of the women over 65 were widows. Nearly 700,000 women lose their husbands each year and will be widows for an average of 14 years(U.S. Bureau of the Census).

✳ The average monthly benefit for non-disabled widow(er)s was $812 in February 2000 (Social Security Administration).

---

9. Found at www.unmarried.org

✳ In 1999 there were over four times as many widows (8.4 million) as widowers (1.9 million).

As with the single, the widow possesses a wealth of life experiences that will enhance your social gathering—in the beginning of the grieving process she may not be the life of the party, but your invitation, extended with a heart of impartiality, may allow her recovery process to accelerate. Remember, as a believer you are instructed to be sensitive and compassionate to the pain and sorrows of others (Rom. 12:15; Col. 3:12)— and there is a 50/50 chance that one day you will be in the same situation (Gal. 6:7)!

Food Security is a twenty-first century term that describes whether or not an individual has access, at all times, to enough food for an active, healthy life; we are more than likely familiar with terms like *low income, poverty level* or *the homeless*—which describe *food insecurity*. This term should touch your heart when you consider that our Lord Jesus, during His earthly ministry, was in essence a homeless person (Matt. 8:20; 2 Cor. 8:9).

According to the USDA *Hunger Report*:

✳ Eighty nine percent of American households were *food secure* throughout 2002.

✳ The remaining households were *food insecure* for at least some time during that year.

✳ The prevalence of *food insecurity* rose from 10.7 percent in 2001 to 11.1 percent in 2002, while the prevalence of *food insecurity* with hunger rose from 3.3 percent to 3.5 percent.

While our pantries may not always be filled with all of the delicacies that our palates might desire, most of us have an adequate enough food supply to be considered *food secure*; we can embrace impartiality by designating a portion of our food budget each month to those who encounter *food insecurity*.

Your opportunities to display impartiality are literally limitless; however, if you are going to make your faith practical you will consider:

* nurturing the abandoned—we will discuss orphans in the response to another question (Exod. 2:6-10).

* providing material needs (2 Sam. 17:27-29).

* weeping, mourning, praying and, when appropriate, fasting for others (Neh. 1:1-11).

* sharing your faith with the spiritually bankrupt (Matt. 11:28-30).

* encouraging the weak and oppressed (Isa. 40:11, 42:3; Matt. 12:18-21).

* assisting with the needs of the infirm (Luke 7:13; John 11:33, 35).

* modeling Biblical compassion (Mark 8:1-2).

Align Your Thoughts

As you reflect on food insecurity consider that one day your life's circumstances may plunge you into poverty or homelessness. If that were to happen, would you be like my friend Melinda whose graciousness and impartiality provided her with a support group drawn from a wide assortment of ages, professional standings and social circles? I challenge you, through the strength of the Lord, to make a concerted effort to fulfill the royal law (James 2:8-10.).

45. What Can I Learn About God from Orphans?

A blond-haired, blue-eyed daughter, she looked like the perfect blend of her mother and father. As others commented on the likeness, the new parents smiled inwardly knowing that it was their heavenly Father who had made this match as He had 'made a home for the lonely' (NASB) or, according to the King James Version, had set another solitary in a family (Ps. 68:6). Older when they commenced the adoption process, Oliver and Mary Ennis welcomed to their home an abandoned child with pneumonia. She had lain so long on her back that her head was bald. You may not realise that I was that abandoned child.

Celebrations were important in the Ennis home. I recall well the January afternoon when I arrived at home and found the dining room table set with Mom's best linen and china. Lying across my bed was a new 'fancy' dress. My favorite black patent leather shoes were awaiting my feet. I was ten. I was helped to dress for dinner. Dad arrived, stayed in his best suit and a special dinner was served. He then began the explanation for the celebration—January 31st was the day that they had brought me home from the hospital, six months after my birth. I was not their birth child but was very special because they had chosen me. That evening we were celebrating the day that I joined the Ennis family. Without giving me extensive details—my parents explained many things to me but did not feel obligated to try to make a child understand all adult decisions. However, my father's explanation of my adoption made the subsequent transition to salvation smooth. Salvation was like being adopted into God's family. How could I not desire heavenly adoption when my earthly adoption was so wonderful?

Adoption Theology

The biblical basis for adoption is concisely stated in James 1:27, 'Religion that is pure and undefiled before God and the Father is this: to visit orphans and widows in their affliction, and to keep oneself unstained from the world.' John MacArthur writes,

> James picks two synonymous adjectives to define the most spotless kind of religious faith—that which is measured by compassionate love (cf. John 13:35), orphans and widows. Those without parents or husbands were and are an especially needy segment of the church. Since they are usually unable to reciprocate in any way, caring for them clearly demonstrates true, sacrificial, Christian love.[10]

Adoption, by definition, means to 'legally take another's child and bring it up as one's own.'[11] Since Christians are, through God's grace, accepted into His family without limitation or restriction they should readily grasp the concept of adoption. Ephesians 1:5 clearly states that 'He predestined us for adoption as sons through Jesus Christ, according to the purpose of his will.' Considering the theological basis of adoption assists the believer in comprehending that the goal of adoption is that the glory of God's grace may be exhibited.

Adoption imagery is infused throughout the New Testament. John 1:12-13 affirms, 'But to all who did receive

---

10. John MacArthur, *The MacArthur Study Bible* (Nashville: Word, 2000), notes at James 1:27: orphans and widows.

11. *Random House Webster's College Dictionary*, 2nd ed., s.v. 'adoption'.

him, who believed in his name, he gave the right to become children of God, who were born, not of blood nor of the will of the flesh nor of the will of man, but of God.' Writing to the Romans, Paul states:

> For you did not receive the spirit of slavery to fall back into fear, but you have received the Spirit of adoption as sons, by whom we cry, 'Abba! Father!' The Spirit himself bears witness with our spirit that we are children of God, and if children, then heirs—heirs of God, and fellow heirs with Christ, provided we suffer with him in order that we may also be glorified with him (Rom. 8:15-17).

Examples of adoption, or something parallel to it, are woven throughout Scripture:

* Moses was essentially adopted by Pharaoh's daughter (Exod. 2:1-10).

* Samuel was left in the care of Eli the high priest rather than being nurtured by his biological mother, Hannah (1 Sam. 1:1–2:21).

* Esther was adopted as a child by her adult cousin, Mordecai (Esther 2:7).

* Jesus was nurtured by His stepfather, Joseph of Nazareth (Luke 2:4, 41-50).

* All believers are taken from their natural master, the Devil, and adopted into God's eternal family (Gal. 4:3-7).

The placement of these solitary individuals into families was a part of God's sovereign plan. A journey through the Scriptures teaches us that:

✳ There is significant financial and emotional expense associated with human adoption. However, those expenses are insignificant when compared with the costliness of a believer's adoption into God's eternal family (Gal. 3:13, 4:4-5).

✳ The process of legal adoption requires careful planning and execution of a myriad of legal formalities. This detailed process is a reminder that the heavenly Father planned far in advance for our adoption—He predestined us for adoption before the creation of the world (Eph. 1:4-6).

✳ Most children available for adoption need to be rescued from precarious situations. Often they are difficult to deal with. Such was our state when God adopted you and me. Adoption is a reminder that by nature we are *children of wrath* (Eph. 2:3). Though the distance between who God is and what we are is great, He still chooses to adopt us into His family.

✳ Legally adopted children have the privilege of receiving full rights of inheritance from their parents. This legal privilege prompts believers to recall that as children of God we become His heirs (Gal. 4:6-7). God appointed His Son to be heir of all things (Heb. 1:2). Every child adopted into God's family is a joint heir with Christ (Rom. 8:16-17).

The concept of placing the solitary in families has strong implications for the twenty-first century Christian community.

Adoption Implications for the Twenty-First Century Christian Community

Adoption is an issue that is on the heart of God. Reflecting again on James 1:27, you are reminded that 'religion that is pure and undefiled before God and the Father is this:

to visit orphans and widows in their affliction'. Practically speaking this means reaching down to the abandoned person who is helpless and may die without our physical care and spiritual nurturing.

Orphans teach you about the love of God, call you to sacrifice and challenge you to value Christ-likeness above your comfort. Not everyone is called to adopt, but within the Christian community there are probably more individuals who should consider it. Orphan Sunday is 2 November. As the date approaches are you willing to ask your heavenly Father, 'What do you have for me in relation to adoption?' His response might just change the course of your life.

46. Do I Walk Worthy of My Profession?

If there is one place that we need to be proficient at multi-tasking it is in our professional employment—whether in the corporate world or at home! Secular literature tells us we must multi-task and at the same time prove ourselves worthy of the profession we are pursuing. It then provides a myriad of suggestions: dress for success, stay on the cutting edge, be assertive, don't bump your head on the glass ceiling, etc.

What do you think of when you consider walking worthy of your profession? As a believer I am most concerned about its biblical definition because I want those I encounter to be drawn to my heavenly Father by my professional performance. Let's consider what Scripture has to say about the topic.

The Apostle Paul opens the fourth chapter of Ephesians with the challenge, '...walk in a manner worthy of the calling to which you have been called ...' Before we look at some specific qualities of the *worthy walk*, let's take a few moments for personal evaluation, beginning with the skills and abilities God bestowed upon you—does your daily conduct reflect that you are a careful steward of them? What is your *profession*? Do you know its purpose and aims? Are you excited about the impact you can make to this *profession* as a Christian? Very early in my Christian walk my mentor, Verna Birkey, taught me a motto that has consistently motivated my *professional* behavior—'I am a personal representative of the living God, on assignment to make God visible to others around me.' As you function in your *profession* is your heavenly Father evident to those who interface with you?

A variety of qualities will be evident in our lives if we are leading a life worthy of our divine calling.. We have already discussed the importance of *excellence* being our standard in all of our endeavors; quite simply, *excellence* is the level we are to attempt to achieve as we serve our Lord in our professions. We are also to be an example to others; regardless of our position, we must not demand that others reach a standard of performance that we are unwilling to embrace. Whether in the marketplace or the home, we are to model the behaviors we expect others to practice.

One of the greatest sources of accountability in my professional walk is my students. When I leave the classroom I climb eighteen stairs and walk twenty-five steps from my classroom to my office. Throughout the day my students observe whether or not the character principles I teach them are important enough to me to implement them in my interaction with others. They hear how I answer my phone, discern my attitude when I am interrupted and observe how I interact with my Faculty,

Administrative Assistant, a variety of campus workers and guests. Throughout the day I can either reinforce or negate my classroom instruction. Following the Apostle Paul's instruction, I daily seek to live with the attitude and practice of *humility, gentleness* and *patience* while I *bear with others in love* and maintain a *unity of spirit.*

Humility is the most foundational Christian virtue and is the quality of character commanded in the first beatitude, Matthew 5:3; being *poor in spirit* (humble) is the opposite of self-sufficiency. This speaks of the deep humility of recognizing one's utter spiritual bankruptcy apart from God. It describes those who are acutely conscious of their own lostness and hopelessness apart from divine grace. *Gentleness* is an inevitable product of humility and refers to that which is mild-spirited and self-controlled, while *patience* means long-tempered and refers to a resolved patience that is an outgrowth of *humility* and *gentleness. Bearing with others in love* requires the application of *humility, gentleness* and *patience.* The evidence of my application of this quality is demonstrated when I choose to maintain self-control when I am subjected to annoyance or provocation. It is my choice to continue to offer unconditional love even when others are acting in a way that would make it easy to withdraw my love.

At times our Lord will place a student in our department who stretches my love; He has taught me to first examine the situation carefully—am I irritated because I am seeing a mirror image of my behaviors and I don't like what I see? Or is He challenging me to practice the truth of 1 Peter 4:8, 'to have fervent love for one another'(NKJV)? *Fervent* means 'to be stretched', 'to be strained'. It is used of a runner who is moving at maximum output with taut muscles straining and stretching to the limit. This kind of love requires the Christian to put another's spiritual good ahead of his own desires in spite of being treated unkindly, ungraciously or even with hostility. As I choose to *bear with others* and make allowances for them rather than becoming annoyed or provoked, I am demonstrating my love for them, even when I don't love their behavior! Paul also reminds me that I am to eagerly and earnestly seek to 'preserve the unity of the Spirit in the bond of peace' (Eph. 4:3 NIV). Let's look at four keys to successfully practice the *worthy walk*.

The Apostle Paul presents four keys to the *worthy walk* in Philippians 3:12-14 that provide direction to the twenty-first century Multi-tasked Woman: a genuine restlessness (Phil. 3:12), a solitary longing (Phil. 3:13), a wholehearted purpose (Phil. 3:12, 14), and a definite goal (Phil. 3:13, 14).

Paul's *genuine restlessness* is a model for all believers; while he was satisfied with his Savior and his salvation, he was dissatisfied with his flesh—he was restless with his spiritual status because he was not all that he knew that he could or should be. 'Paul uses the analogy of a runner to describe the Christian's spiritual growth. The believer has not reached his goal of Christlikeness, but like the runner in a race, he must continue to pursue it.'[12] The Christian life is to be exciting—and as multi-tasked women we should be excited about growing, regardless of our spiritual age.

Paul's *solitary longing* helps us to eliminate the unnecessary from our lives. Our quest toward Christlikeness

---

12. John MacArthur, *The MacArthur Study Bible* (Nashville: Word, 1997), note at 1 Peter 4:8 fervent love.

puts life into a single focus—Paul says, 'this *one* thing I do'. As Multi-tasked Women we are to have only one goal—to serve God with our entire being (Mark 12:30; Col. 3:17). Our Lord Jesus serves as the ultimate role model for this *solitary longing*. 'He did not finish all the urgent tasks in Palestine or all the things He would have liked to do, but He did finish the work God gave Him to do. The only alternative to frustration is to be sure that we are doing what God wants. Nothing substitutes for knowing that this day, this hour, in this place we are doing the will of the Father. Then and only then can we think of all the other unfinished tasks with equanimity and leave them with God.'[13]

Paul's *wholehearted purpose* helped him to focus on his determination to keep moving toward the goal. We will not succeed if we do not have a strong determination, but its source must be executed in the strength of the Holy Spirit, not simply our sheer determination (Phil. 4:13). As Christian women, are we mature enough to keep pursuing our 'upward call' (Phil. 3:14) when it would be easier to quit?

Finally, Paul had a *definite goal*, and he moved toward it with tenacity. Serving God with our entire being challenges us to refuse to dwell on the past—regardless of whether it is filled with success or sin. What we are today is what counts! Paul challenges us to refuse to drink from the cup of self-pity and to release past grudges and incidents of mistreatment—he forgot these and died climbing!

---

13. Charles Hummel, *Tyranny Of The Urgent* (Downers Grove: Intervarsity, 1967), 15.

Now that we have established a biblical foundation for our worthy walk, it's time to identify some practical suggestions for implementing Christian integrity on the job.

✳ Learn the chain of command in your organization and focus on submitting to those in authority. Remember that submission is willingly placing one's self under someone else's direction. As employees we have a responsibility to respond positively to our leadership unless they ask us to fulfill a request that violates Scripture.

✳ Build an appropriate, positive relationship with your superiors. Look for ways to make them successful.

✳ Seek to establish positive relationships with co-workers. Romans 12:18 encourages us to do everything possible to work in harmony with others; if disharmony surfaces it should be the result of others' negative attitudes and responses, not yours.

✳ Study the politics of the organization, but stay away from involvement in organizational politics. If you are unavoidably drawn into a political situation attempt to remain neutral.

✳ Refrain from criticizing the organization and the people in it. Choosing to think about what is good about it is a practical way to implement Philippians 4:8-9 into your daily life.

✳ Avoid becoming part of a clique, and, as a new employee, don't team up with one person in the group too soon.

✳ Avoid being caught in the 'everyone else is doing it' syndrome.

✳ Dress professionally, always giving priority to the principles of modesty presented in 1 Timothy 2:9-10 and 1 Peter 3:3-6.

✳ Be a good steward of the organization's resources and display integrity when using them—for example, refrain from conducting personal business on company time and don't use company supplies for personal use.

✳ Grow graciously in your professional role. Proverbs 11:16 reminds us 'a gracious woman gets honor'. This means not misusing others to achieve your goals and not flaunting your achievements. There is no advancement that is worth sacrificing your Christian reputation.

✳ Remember that you are the member of a team; recalling the definition of the word TEAM—Together Everyone Achieves More—will help you focus on making your best contribution without trying to control every situation.

✳ Keep focused on the fact that the organization existed before you arrived and will more than likely survive after your departure. When you are in a position of leadership make changes gradually—this strategy generally reduces animosity.

✳ Be the best employee you can be—purpose to function at a level of proficiency that reflects you are 'walking worthy of your profession', practice flexibility, cultivate an attitude of contentment, solicit feedback from others, don't become defensive when others offer suggestions for improvement and always project a teachable spirit.

✳ Share your faith by modeling it; communicate it on your own time, not your organization's.

✳ Remember that your performance in this position is the foundation for our Lord's next assignment for you—make sure it is a solid one!

If we are to visualize our profession as a high calling we will choose to delight ourselves in the Lord (Ps. 37:4-5); this means that our multi-tasking will include wholeheartedly serving our Lord at all times, in all places and in all situations.

47. Who Are My Role Models?

Who are your role models? Perhaps you have several in your life—one role model may excel professionally, another in raising children, another in hospitality and yet another in Bible knowledge. Though I have a number of earthly role models, some of my most significant ones come from women of the Old and New Testament. Early in my spiritual growth I leaned that I could eliminate much spiritual and emotional turmoil from my life by examining the lives of the men and women who walk through the pages of Scripture. I could learn from both their successes and failures (1 Cor. 10:1-12). I carry this knowledge into the college classroom and assign my students studies of women of the Old and New Testament each time I teach the class that includes the study of Proverbs 31:10-31. I still recall the young widow from Africa who came to the college to further her education. She was a relatively new believer and had as her responsibility her young son and brother. After several weeks of classes she held up her textbook, and with tears in her eyes shared with the class:'This is my first Bible study book, and through it I have learned to read the Bible as a woman—I am beginning to understand that my heavenly Father loves women!' She summarized in those few words my passion for meeting the women of the Bible personally.

Let me introduce you to three female role models from scripture: Mary, Martha and Dorcas. As we seek to impact our world for our Lord each offer positive and negative character qualities for us to emulate or avoid. This will help us as we seek to be servant leaders, the Biblical approach to impacting our world for eternity (Mark 10:44-45). A servant leader models Mark 10:44-45 by becoming excited about making others successful—and that means she is more concerned about the achievements of others than her own advancement. This concept is beautifully captured in the classic children's story, *The Velveteen Rabbit* …

> The Skin Horse had lived longer in the nursery than any of the others. He was so old that his brown coat was bald in patches and showed the seams underneath, and most of the hairs in his tail had been pulled out to string bead necklaces. He was wise, for he had seen a long succession of mechanical toys arrive to boast and swagger, and by-and-by break their mainsprings and pass away, and he knew that they were only toys, and would never turn into anything else. For nursery magic is very strange and wonderful, and only those playthings that are old and wise and experienced like the Skin Horse understand all about it.
>
> 'What is REAL?' asked the Rabbit one day, when they were lying side by side near the nursery fender, before Nana came to tidy the room. 'Does it mean having things that buzz inside you and a stick-out handle?'
>
> 'Real isn't how you are made,' said the Skin Horse. 'It's a thing that happens to you. When a child loves you for a long, long time, not just to play with, but REALLY love you, then you become real.'
>
> 'Does it hurt?' asked the Rabbit.
>
> 'Sometimes,' said the Skin Horse, for he was always truthful. 'When you are Real you don't mind being hurt.'

'Does it happen all at once, like being wound up,' he asked, 'or bit by bit?'

'It doesn't happen all at once,' said the Skin Horse. 'You become. It takes a long time. That's why it doesn't often happen to people who break easily, or have sharp edges, or who have to be carefully kept. Generally, by the time you are Real, most of your hair has been loved off, and your eyes drop out and you get loose in the joints and very shabby. But these things don't matter at all, because once you are real you can't be ugly, except to people who don't understand.'[14]

As you contemplate your life, are you willing to allow our Lord to shape your character so that as you approach retirement age you are considered *real?*

Seven verses describe the three women who contribute to our composite role model; four are dedicated to Mary and Martha (Luke 10:38-42) and three to Dorcas (Acts 9:36-39). Mary's example teaches us our first priority as Multi-tasked Women—that of spending time with our Lord so that we are prepared to serve Him effectively. Luke 10:39 describes Mary as sitting at Jesus' feet and savoring His instructions. Mary sat long enough to listen to her Master before she performed a task that potentially had a long-term impact (Mark 14:1-10). Do our efforts produce short-term results or long-term impact? As I contemplate the response to this question I am reminded of Steve Green's song, 'Find Us Faithful'. When my Lord calls me home or He comes for me, what evidence of my faith will others find when they sort through my belongings? Will they be

---

14. Margery Williams, *The Velveteen Rabbit* (New York: Doubleday and Company, Inc., 1958), 16-17.

drawn to the One that loved me and redeemed me or will they only be impressed by organizational and management skills? And when I meet my Lord, will He say of me, 'Pat, you chose the good portion, which will not be taken away from you (Luke 10:42)'? These questions motivate me to pray daily that I will choose to first embrace Mary's model.

Martha's word portrait reveals the second priority of multi-tasking: learning to make good decisions. Martha was a woman who could think on her feet—notice that she was quick to extend hospitality to her Lord and His disciples. Luke 10:38 describes Martha as welcoming Him into her house—an admirable quality for all of us to emulate. However, Luke 10:40 suggests that though Martha had the right idea, the intensity of her approach to her responsibilities merited some softening. 'Distracted literally means "dragging all around"; the expression implies that Martha was in a tumult *with much serving*—that she was fussing about with details that were unnecessarily elaborate.'[15] And what about the results of her fussing? She quickly developed a negative attitude toward Mary (Luke 10:40) and was rebuked rather than affirmed by the One she wanted to please. We learn from Martha's life that she was successful in getting things done, making things happen and clearly articulating her thoughts—all qualities that a Multi-tasking Woman desires. Blending Martha's efficiency attributes with Mary's tender spirit yields a powerful tool for our Lord's service—however it is only attainable as we allow Him to manage our lives.

---

15. John MacArthur, *The MacArthur Study Bible* (Nashville: Word, 1997), notes at Luke 10:40 distracted ... with much serving.

The Valley of Vision, A Collection of Puritan Prayers and Devotions is a small book with a profound message. Its contents draw the reader back to 'the largely forgotten deposit of Puritan spiritual exercises, meditations and aspirations'.[16] The prayer entitled 'Regeneration' reflects the influence that our Lord desires to have over the Martha portion of our character ...

REGENERATION

O GOD OF THE HIGHEST HEAVEN,
Occupy the throne of my heart,
take full possession and reign supreme,
lay low every rebel lust,
let no vile passion resist thy holy war;
manifest thy mighty power,
and make me thine for ever.
Thou art worthy to be
praised with my every breath,
loved with my every faculty of soul,
served with my every act of life.
Thou has loved me, espoused me, received me,
purchased, washed, favored, clothed, adorned me,
when I was worthless, vile, soiled, polluted.
I was dead in iniquities,
having no eyes to see thee,
no ears to hear thee,
no taste to relish thy joys,
no intelligence to know thee;

---

16. Arthur Bennett, editor, *The Valley of Vision, A Collection of Puritan Prayers and Devotions* (Carlisle: The Banner of Truth Trust, 2002), ix.

But thy Spirit has quickened me,
has brought me into a new world as a new creature,
has given me spiritual perception,
has opened to me thy Word as light, guide, solace, joy.
Thy presence is to me a treasure of unending peace;
No provocation can part me from thy sympathy,
for thou has drawn me with cords of love,
and dost forgive me daily, hourly.
O help me then to walk worthy of thy love,
of my hopes, and my vocation.
Keep me, for I cannot keep myself;
Protect me that no evil befall me;
Let me lay aside every sin admired of many;
Help me to walk by thy side, lean on thy arm,
hold converse with thee,
That henceforth I may be salt of the earth
and a blessing to all.[17]

If you were asked who is managing the Martha portion of your character, what would be your response?

The brief description of Dorcas completes our composite role model portrait and provides our third priority: learning to be a disciple. When we hear the name Dorcas we conjure up mental images of the lady who was the seamstress of Joppa— but that's not how she is introduced. Acts 9:36 presents her as a *disciple*—the only woman in the Bible honored with that description. '*Disciple* means "student", one who is being taught by another.'[18] Though we do not know who taught Dorcas,

---

17. Ibid., 84-85.
18. John MacArthur, *The MacArthur Study Bible* (Nashville: Word, 1997), notes at Matthew 10:1 **disciples**.

we do know that she possessed a teachable spirit because she was described as a disciple. We also know that she was 'abounding with deeds of charity, which she continually did' (Acts 9:36 NASB). This would indicate that her teaching impacted her heart as well as her head, and motivated kind actions rather than simply making her arrogant (1 Cor. 8:1). As we evaluate our professional experiences are we, as Multi-tasked Women, willing to learn from others? How does our accumulation of knowledge and training affect us—do we become arrogant, or does each phase of our professional and spiritual development motivate us to greater acts of kindness?

Dorcas was willing to use the skill she had to minister to the needs of others. So should we. Her profession, according to Acts 9:39, was that of seamstress to a specific clientele—widows. Are we generous with those who are the recipients of our talents or are we a respecter of persons (James 2:1-13)? And are we quick to be careful stewards of the knowledge and skills that we have, or do we place a high price tag on them, minimize their importance, or choose to 'hide them under a bushel'?

We began with asking if one of your goals as a multi-tasking Christian woman is to be both salt and light to a decaying world. The lives of Mary, Martha and Dorcas challenge us to maintain four priorities:

* spending time with our Lord so that we are prepared to serve Him effectively.

* learning to make good decisions.

* having a teachable spirit (becoming a disciple).

* possessing a willingness to use our skills to minister to the needs of others.

To effectively multi-task, these priorities are to be motivated by a heart of love rather than for selfish fulfillment (Gal. 5:13). Often, however, the application of the principles begins with an act of the will—that is doing the right thing and then allowing our emotions to catch-up with us (remember the entire book of Psalms is directed to our will, not our emotions). As you multi-task will you ask your heavenly Father to conform your will to His so that you are salt and light to a decaying world?

48. How Can I Evaluate My Spiritual Growth?

As you progressed through *God Is My Strength*, you spent time in your heavenly Father's company cultivating character qualities that contributed to your understanding that God is always your strength. If you chose to allow the unchanging Word of God to be consistently applied to your life, when faced with life's challenges you became a victor rather than a victim. It is now time to evaluate the impact of this study. I invite you to prayerfully consider the following questions and respond by recording in a journal your visible growth towards acknowledging that you can do all things through God's strength!

DO I ...

✳ filter my daily decisions through the changeless instructions found in God's Word (Ps. 119:9-16)?

✳ consistently express my gratitude to those who are willing to serve as my mentors (1 Thess. 5:18)?

✳ allow the testing of my faith to produce deeper communion and greater trust in Christ (James 1:2-5)?

207

* choose to exhibit spiritual vitality regardless of the circumstances (Jer. 17:7-8)?

* desire to be a faithful steward of the gifts my heavenly Father gave me (Matt. 25:14-30; 1 Peter 4:10)?

* approach *s-t-r-e-t-c-h-i-n-g* experiences believing that I can 'do all things through Christ who strengthens me' (Phil. 4:13)?

* have priorities that reflect an eternal perspective and follow the model of the Lord who glorified His Father while on earth while finishing the work He gave His Son to do (John 17:4)?

* deliberately bring thoughts of little or big needs to Christ's control (2 Cor. 10:5)?

* choose the *Elijah Effect* or embrace contentment when faced with circumstances that could breed discouragement (Rom. 8:18-39)?

* seek to fulfill 'the royal law according to the Scriptures', and love my neighbor as myself (Matt. 22:37-40)?

* use Scripture to replace my fear of man with the knowledge that God is sufficient to override my fears (Ps. 56:3, 11)?

* acknowledge that God's brand of modesty is always in style (1 Tim. 2:9)?

* use my days of singleness to concentrate on becoming complete in Christ (Col. 3:10)?

* base my sense of worth on the unchanging standard of God's Word rather than the propaganda of the world (Isa. 43:21; 2 Cor. 4:7)?

* purpose to forgive even when I am maligned, neglected and unappreciated (Luke 23:34)?

* joyfully embrace God's special instructions relating to spiritual motherhood (Titus 2:3-5)?

* choose to honor my parents by affirming their positive character qualities (Phil. 4:8-9)? Do I view their weaknesses through the lens that each possesses a potential strength and pray that they will choose to allow the Lord to transform those weaknesses to strengths (Mark 10:27)?

* purpose to be an imitator of God (Matt. 5:48; Eph. 5:1; 1 Pet. 1:15-16)?

* offer trust and confidence in my friendships (Prov. 17:17)?

* make time in my schedule for female companionship (Eccles. 4:9-12)?

* extend kindness, forgive (Eph. 4:32), bear with weaknesses and idiosyncrasies (Gal. 6:1-2), and reassure my friends (1 Thess. 5:14)?

* intentionally eradicate the weeds from my Friendship Garden (James 4:6)?

* regularly evaluate the quality of friendship I extend to others (1 Cor. 10:31)?

* entertain or practice biblical hospitality (Rom. 12:13b; 1 Tim. 3:1-2; Titus 1:7-8; Heb. 13:2; 1 Pet. 4:9; 3 John 7-8)?

Once the evaluation is completed consider prayerfully crafting specific goals that will motivate your growth toward the continued mindset that God is always your strength. As well, consider studying the life of Rahab who allowed God to polish her marred reputation so that at the conclusion of her life she was worthy to be one of the two women recorded in the gallery of the heroes and heroines of faith (Josh. 2:1-21, 6:22-25; James 2:25; Heb. 11:30-31).

49. Do You Really Believe What You Wrote in this Book?

You will recall from the Introduction, *God is My Strength* was designed to allow you to spend time in your heavenly Father's company cultivating character qualities that contribute to your trusting God for your daily strength. The responses to the fifty questions comprising the book's contents were drawn from the spiritual challenges that I, as well as women I have taught and counseled through my spiritual pilgrimage, confront. As the unchanging Word of God is applied to our lives, we become victors rather than victims—and in the process experience growth toward comprehending that God is *always* our strength (Ps. 29:11).

Early in my teaching ministry I was amazed to discover that my students thought I was teaching conceptually rather than experientially about the topics contained within the covers of this book. You see, I was reluctant to spend valuable class time talking about myself until one day a young woman walked into my office and bluntly stated, 'I really don't know why I am here to talk with you; you see I have so many personal challenges in my life, and I truly need someone to counsel with me. However, I don't think you will understand, since your life has always been so perfect!' As she poured out her heart to me, it was as if I were looking in a mirror—her life experiences almost exactly paralleled mine. It was then I realized that I needed to share that much of what I taught was the result of the lessons I had learned from my heavenly Father. Perhaps what I shared with her about the seasons of my life will encourage you that though you may not always feel your heavenly Father's presence, as His dear child, He never leaves you or forsakes you (Heb. 13:5b).

The Season of Divine Protection

I was abandoned by my birth parents; when my mother left the hospital, I stayed.

During the first six months of my life I battled pneumonia, and though I was unaware of my heavenly Father's presence, His promise of Psalm 68:5-6 that He would be a 'father of the fatherless ... and that He sets the solitary in families' (NASB) was functioning in my life. He deemed that six months later I would be adopted into a Christian family, and at the age of ten I would learn, in Vacation Bible School, that salvation was like being adopted into God's family. It was His plan that the specialness of my first adoption would cause me to eagerly become His daughter!

In the Season of Divine Protection My
Heavenly Father was my strength!

The Season of Reinforcement

My heavenly Father knew that my church taught salvation each Sunday but did not teach me how to grow as His child. He also knew that I carried the burden of sick parents and many challenges, rather than casting them on Him (1 Pet. 5:6-8). The death of my parents—my Father when I was eighteen and my Mother when I was twenty-three— was no surprise to Him, and He made Hebrews 13:5, 'I will never leave you, nor will I ever forsake you', a reality in my life.

In the Season of Reinforcement My
Heavenly Father was my strength!

The Season of Growth

My heavenly Father led me to Scott Memorial Baptist Church where, under the ministry of Pastor Tim LaHaye, He confronted me with my sin and showed me through His Word that I must repent of it, trust in Jesus for salvation and submit to Him as Lord (Rom. 10:9). I agreed with His declaration that Jesus is Savior and Lord (Rom. 10:10) and thus had my salvation confirmed (Rom. 10:13).

In the Season of Growth My Heavenly
Father was my strength!

The Season of Spiritual Reproduction

My heavenly Father knows that from the date of that commitment I have daily sought His guidance and desire to 'walk in the Spirit, and not fulfill the lust of the flesh' (Gal. 5:16). I gladly responded to Him as Mary did when she said, 'Behold the maidservant of the Lord! Let it be according to Your Word' (Luke 1:38), by serving Him full-time in Christian Higher Education for the majority of my professional career. He knew that I could serve Him more effectively as a single woman and has consistently provided all of my spiritual, physical and emotional needs (1 Cor. 7:7-8, Phil. 4:19). One day He will welcome me to heaven because I am His daughter simply coming home!

In the Season of Spiritual Reproduction My
Heavenly Father continues to be my strength!

As we conclude our time together may I encourage you to record the Seasons of your life and God's faithfulness to you so that, when He welcomes you home, He will affirm that you trusted Him to be your strength each day of your earthly journey?

Thanks for joining me for the Journey,

Pat ☺

Psalm 28

50. A Final Thought

As we walked through the pages of *God is My Strength* together it was my passion to share with you responses to questions that women frequently pose that would challenge you to become theologically sound (Titus 2:1-5) as well as a 'doer of the word' (James 1:22) in the critical areas of your life ...

Your God
Yourself
Your Relationships
Your Home
Your World

As we conclude our journey may I encourage you to embrace the examples of women of the Bible who embraced God as their strength with a determined mindset? Begin by stating:

I WILL, LIKE ...

The Queen of Sheba, diligently seek godly wisdom
(1 Kings 10:1-13)

Ruth, respond to the advice of older women
(Ruth 3:5)

Sarah, submit to those in authority over me
(1 Pet. 3:6)

The little Jewish Maid, boldly but
appropriately speak of my faith
(2 Kings 5:1-14)

Esther, choose to take risks to further God's kingdom
(Esther 4:1-17)

The Widow of Zarephath, trust my heavenly
Father to multiply my resources
(1 Kings 17:10-24)

The ShunammiteWoman, extend hospitality
(2 Kings 4:8-37)

Mary, the Mother of Jesus, wholeheartedly declare
myself a bondslave of the Lord
(Luke 1:26-38)

Elizabeth, believe that God works
miracles in women of all ages
(Luke 1:5-25)

Mary of Bethany, listen with a teachable spirit
to My Master's Words
(Luke 10:38-41)

The poor widow, give out of my need rather
than my abundance
(Mark 12:42)

Mary, exhibit humble love and devotion for my Lord
(John 12:2-3)

Dorcas, share my talents with those in need
(Acts 9:36-43)

Lydia, choose to use my profession
for my Lord's glory
(Acts 16:14, 40)

Lois and Eunice, endeavor to leave a godly heritage
(2 Tim. 1:5)

The Multi-tasked Woman of Proverbs,
purpose to fear my Lord
(Prov. 31:10-31)

Realizing that I cannot hope to achieve these
goals in my own strength
I will rely upon my Lord ... for I can do all things
through Christ who strengthens me
(Phil. 4:13)

It is my prayer that the tidbits of wisdom contained in *God is My Strength* provided you a foundation for a life-long quest for *wisdom* and stimulated a spiritual appetite within you to embrace, with joy, the biblical challenge to acquire godly *wisdom* and apply *understanding* to your heart (Prov. 2). Blessings to you as you continue embrace the truth that God is your strength!

Meditation Thoughts on My World

The woman who trusts God as her strength …

✳ develops a worldview.

✳ desires to be both salt and light to a decaying world (Matt. 5:13-16).

✳ acknowledges that she will be judged on the quality of her work (1 Cor. 3:13, 4:5; 2 Cor. 5:10; Rev. 20:12).

✳ does her work with enthusiasm—as unto her Lord, not simply to please others (Col. 3:23).

✳ develops an *excellent* standard of professional conduct (Eph. 4:1).

✳ daily seeks to live with the attitude and practice of *humility, gentleness, and patience* while she *bears with others in love* and maintains a *unity of spirit* (Eph. 4:2).

✳ is excited about growing, regardless of her chronological age (Phil. 3:12).

✳ eliminates the unnecessary from her life (Phil. 3:13).

✳ keeps pursuing her 'upward call' when it would be easier to quit (Phil. 3:14).

✳ wholeheartedly serves her Lord at all times, in all places and in all situations (Ps. 37:4-5).

✳ develops gracious behavior (Prov. 11:16).

✳ examines the lives of the men and women who walk through the pages of Scripture and learns from both their successes and failures (1 Cor. 10:1-12).

✳ embraces the examples of the multi-tasked women of the Bible with a determined mindset (Phil. 4:13).

Building My Spiritual Stamina

Continually think about or contemplate the Scriptures that focus your mind on those things that are true, noble, right, pure, lovely, and admirable (cf. PHIL. 4:8)

Like a gold ring in a pig's snout,
is a beautiful woman without discretion.
PROVERBS 11:22

Sing praises to the Lord,
For he has done graciously;
Let this be made known in all the earth.
ISAIAH 12:5

And as you wish that others would do to you,
do so to them.
LUKE 6:31

I therefore, a prisoner for the Lord,
Urge you to walk in a manner worthy of the calling to which
you have been called,
With all humility and gentleness,
With patience, bearing with one another in love,
Eager to maintain the unity of the spirit in the bond of peace.
EPHESIANS 4:1-3

Not that I have already obtained this or am already perfect,
But I press on to make it my own,
Because Christ Jesus has made me his own.

Brothers, I do not consider that I have made it my own.
But one thing I do:
Forgetting what lies behind and straining
forward to what lies ahead.
I press on toward the goal for the
prize of the upward call of God
In Christ Jesus.
PHILIPPIANS 3:12-14

Let the word of Christ dwell in you richly,
teaching and admonishing one another in all wisdom,
singing psalms and hymns and spiritual songs,
with thankfulness in your hearts to God.
And whatever you do, in word or deed,
do everything in the name of the Lord Jesus,
giving thanks to God the Father through him.
COLOSSIANS 3:16-17

And so, from the day we heard,
we have not ceased to pray for you,
asking that you may be filled with the
knowledge of his will in all
spiritual wisdom and understanding,
so as to walk in a manner worthy of the Lord,
fully pleasing to him, bearing fruit in every good work and
increasing in the knowledge of God.
COLOSSIANS 1:9-10

Sustaining My Spiritual Stamina

Further study to encourage renewal of your
mind and spirit (cf. EPH. 4:17-32)

＊ Evaluate John 10:10 in light of the question, 'How broad is your world?'

＊ The lives of Mary, Martha and Dorcas challenge us to maintain four priorities—

> spending time with our Lord so that we are prepared to serve Him effectively.

> learning to make good decisions.

> having a teachable spirit (becoming a disciple).

> possessing a willingness to use our skills to minister to the needs of others.

Evaluate your life in relation to each of the priorities by completing a chart like the one below.

PRIORITY	MY DEFINITION OF THE PRIORITY	PERSONAL GOALS I WILL SET TO ACTIVATE THE PRIORITY
Spending time with my Lord.		
Learning to make good decisions.		
Having a teachable spirit.		
Using my skills to minister to the needs of others.		

✳ Using the 'I Will …' portion of this chapter as a model, write your commitment to embrace the examples of the multi-tasked women of the Bible with a determined mindset.

➤ Support each 'I Will …' with scripture.

➤ Ask someone to hold you accountable to fulfilling your commitment.

Also by
Christian Focus Publications

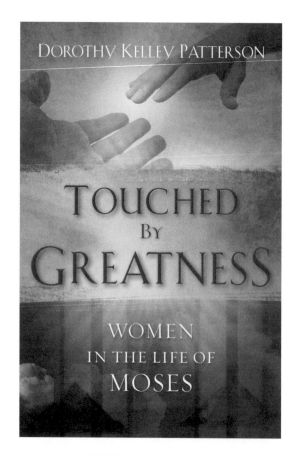

DOROTHY KELLEY PATTERSON

TOUCHED
BY
GREATNESS

WOMEN
IN THE LIFE OF
MOSES

ISBN 978-1-84550-631-5

Touched by Greatness

Women in the life of Moses

DOROTHY K. PATTERSON

Many women impacted upon the life of Moses. The woman who bore him, the young girl who shadowed him, and the foreigner who raised him are just three of the key influencers on his life. Their actions meant that a Hebrew child was reared as a prince of Egypt and became one of the greatest leaders of all time.

Each woman who influenced the life of Moses was guided by God to bring his plans to pass. As you read about their lives you will discover the unique role women have to be mightily used of God too.

Dorothy Patterson is a born Bible teacher and a marvellous mentor for Christian women everywhere. I highly recommend this book.

DENISE GEORGE,
Author, teacher, speaker www.denisegeorge.org

Dorothy Patterson speaks to the very heart of women. In this insightful book you will find a kindred spirit.

DEBBIE BRUNSON,
Pastor's wife, Jacksonville, Florida

Christian Focus Publications

Our mission statement –

STAYING FAITHFUL
In dependence upon God we seek to impact the world through literature faithful to His infallible Word, the Bible. Our aim is to ensure that the Lord Jesus Christ is presented as the only hope to obtain forgiveness of sin, live a useful life and look forward to heaven with Him.

Our books are published in four imprints:

CHRISTIAN FOCUS

Popular works including biographies, commentaries, basic doctrine and Christian living.

CHRISTIAN HERITAGE

Books representing some of the best material from the rich heritage of the church.

MENTOR

Books written at a level suitable for Bible College and seminary students, pastors, and other serious readers. The imprint includes commentaries, doctrinal studies, examination of current issues and church history.

CF4•K

Children's books for quality Bible teaching and for all age groups: Sunday school curriculum, puzzle and activity books; personal and family devotional titles, biographies and inspirational stories – because you are never too young to know Jesus!

Christian Focus Publications Ltd,
Geanies House, Fearn, Ross-shire,
IV20 1TW, Scotland, United Kingdom.
www.christianfocus.com